# HIJACKED

# HIJACKED

## An eyewitness account of evil

# Carole Wells

**MBP**
MotherBird Productions

**MBP**
MotherBird Productions

Published by:
MotherBird Productions

Printed in the United States of America

ISBN Paperback: 978-1-7324909-0-1
ISBN ebook: 978-1-7324909-1-8

Cover design: Diego Tripodi

Interior design: Ghislain Viau

*Thank you to the citizens of Japan, their cabinet members and the Emperor for allowing the nine members of the Japanese Red Army to be released from prison and paying the six million dollars ransom to the hijackers. Without Japan's cooperation the passengers on the Japanese flight 472 might not have survived. I appreciate my fans in Japan for their beautiful gifts and loving notes. I love you all and appreciate how much you did for our release!*

# PROLOGUE

**W**hen you read my story you may think I'm making this up, you may think it is fiction, you may think it's a made-for-TV drama. Well it's not. This account of a plane hijacking really happened to me on my honeymoon forty years ago.

I feel fortunate to have survived through the nightmare in September 1977 when five armed members of the Japanese Red Army commandeered the Paris to Tokyo DC-8 plane that had just left Bombay, forcing it to land in Dhaka, Bangladesh. The terrorists demanded $6 million in cash otherwise each one of the 156 passengers and crew would be executed until their demands were met.

For decades, I tried to forget the agonizing encounter with the power-crazed terrorists that permanently changed my attitude about terror, trust, and life.

I had almost hypnotized myself into suppressing the fear of that horrific week forty years ago until my old wounds were re-opened every time I watched the news on television showing the rampant terrorist attack around the world. I realized my fear was still in me. I must write about my experience to shed light on the existence of sadistic humans who terrorize for control and greed. We Americans must first recognize such hate to work towards promoting peace.

Long before the vicious attacks on innocent people by Al Qaeda and ISIS in 2016 to the present, there was a revolutionary group trained and funded by Yasser Arafat's Palestinian Liberation Organization called the Japanese Red Army. How did Arafat win the Nobel Peace Prize while encouraging hijackings, blowing up planes, and murdering innocent people?

The Japanese Red Army terrorists, JRA, had already proved their taste for blood and violence after the massacre of 26 people at the Ben Gurion Airport in Tel Aviv in May 1972. They murdered innocent passengers on behalf of the PFLP, Popular Front for Liberation of Palestine. Two terrorists died. One survived.

The sadistic JRA leader controlled his ragtag followers with terror, intimidation, brutal torture, and death. The guerrillas had no respect for life and used horrific techniques to maim and terrorize.

These were the men who held my husband, a planeload of passengers and me with threats of massacring us one by one.

This most terrifying experience happened to me and I will strive to relate the events as they happened. Hopefully as I dredge up the events, it will serve as a catharsis to purge the memory from my consciousness.

What would have been a wonderful honeymoon with my new husband put me unwittingly in the middle of twin political crises: a terrorist hijacking of an airplane and a Bangladesh bloody military coup d'état.

This is my story.

# INTRODUCTION

**T**error affects us in many ways. Fear is planted into our subconscious when one is emotionally traumatized. Most people never get over such abuse. I attribute my sanity to my unwavering faith, thanking God every day for allowing me to survive the hijacking. I lived through a horrific experience and emerged a stronger version of myself. The evil I witnessed in that week has never left my mind.

It is time for citizens to empathize with the tortured kidnapped victims and stop ignoring the trend of global terror. There is metastasis cancer growing into a catastrophe. It is time to speak up and fight back!

Most Americans don't feel affected by this terrorist's violence. They watch television, play sports and turn up the music to ignore the tragedies of the world. How can we survive with people not honoring humanity? Why is life so unimportant to

Isis, Al Qaeda, Boko Haram, Hamas, Islamic Jihad, and the Taliban? There are many terrorist organizations all over the world believing that by blowing themselves up they will be granted the riches by their holy Brotherhood and Allah. Now we face a battle of good versus evil. If citizens of the world do not take this violence seriously, our world will be without freedom and peace.

Writing today ignited more anxiety within me. It's hard to see Aleppo devastated as I remember the ancient city in the seventies. I watched the news today and saw the destruction on the Damascus-Aleppo highway, remembering my visit to Kesop. I traveled with Walter Karabian my lawyer, turned lover and a year later became my husband. His Armenian heritage and wanderlust took us to experience the Middle East like very few see today. Wally and I visited Kesop, a remote Armenian community in the mountains near the Turkish border, almost hidden by orchards and the forest. We stayed at a small hotel nestled among the fruit trees where no cars could enter.

The spartan bedroom offered twin beds with rusty springs that poked through the thin mattress. The shower resembled a rusty fishing boat where a chain-pull discharged the water. Wally and I laughed as the shower released a meager stream above the toilet onto our heads. It was primitive and inefficient. Nothing like our American luxuries but we loved every part of it.

At 5:30a.m, just as the lazy gray sky was hurling into a blaze of colors, we were awakened by a woman yelling "Matzoon,

Matzoon." The haunting sounds woke up wives and daughters to buy the fresh yogurt for their daily meals. The seller, an old woman was dressed in a black dress and carried a yoke across her shoulders and on each end was a pail of fresh yogurt. We were served her yogurt at breakfast, paired with fresh fruit and strong coffee. The apples tasted sweet like candy. Their homegrown fruits and vegetables were more refreshing and delicious than what I had ever purchased at our grocery store in Los Angeles.

The villagers had a sweet innocence about them. Satisfied by the simplest of things, they seemed blissfully unaware of all the world's problems. Many of the older generation may never have left their village. I felt thankful for my life in America.

Working in the entertainment industry for most of my life gave me opportunities to travel, meet presidents of countries, royalty and fascinating people from different cultures.

Watching the news on television brings up fears of new terrorist taking away people's freedoms. The tragic part of the story is that most of these people in Kesop were killed. It is the same history of the Armenian genocide of 1915 when 1.5 million Armenians were slaughtered in Turkey. This genocide is very close to the heart of Wally's family as his cousin's father was beheaded and the mother killed on the streets of Istanbul. Terror organizations—Barbarians— stormed in and slaughtered peaceful Christian Armenians because they did not practice Islam. Heads were chopped off, children were raped, civilians turned into slaves until the Al Qauda got tired of them and killed them all. No one survived that innocent village. History just seems to always repeat itself, as the same violence is happening now. Every six minutes a Christian is being killed!

I waited to write my story of being hijacked by the Japanese Red Army because it was so frightening. For years I forced it out of my mind. I thought I was over the fear that haunted me, but no matter how hard one suppresses it, the emotional trauma remains in your cells and memory.

Four years after the hijacking, I went to Aspen. While I was skiing down the slope, I stopped suddenly to allow the machine called a snow-cat to groom the hill. Two men in front of me were smoking and blocking the icy path. I could hear the sounds of their Japanese voices, which instantly sent chills down my spine. At that moment, I broke out into tears and started shaking uncontrollably. My body froze in place for several minutes. It amazed me how much their voices affected me! Even now watching the news killing and kidnapping helpless women and children sends me to bed with horrible dreams and I still wake up feeling terrorized. Just thinking about my hijacking brings up frightening emotions for me. I wish I could say that it didn't affect me in this way but it feels like I need to curl up in a ball and hide.

I recently watched a documentary film by Naeem Mohaiemen, a brilliant Bangledeshi historian whose work has focused on the failed utopias of the revolutionary left during the postcolonial era. This specific documentary film utilizes audio between the terrorists and the government officials to explore the narrative of our hijacking, bringing up more memories of my time in captivity spent on the plane in Dacca, Bangladesh.

Sharing my story I hope to help others understand that people who have been through a terrifying experience like mine are forever traumatized. These actions by a few affect the rest of the world forever, and we must stop terrorism!

I have come to the realization that the hijacking and fear of being executed by the JRA terrorists has haunted me, even though several decades have passed. Medical science has since given the condition a name: Post Traumatic Stress Disorder (PTSD). Although the experience affected me deeply, I never allowed it to stop me from doing the things I love most and persevering through other life challenges.

# CHAPTER ONE

# HONEYMOON

**I** could taste my blood as the terrorist pressed his gun harder against my teeth and gums. My instincts wanted to fight back, but the hand grenade he held in his other hand intimated me.

The man's evil black eyes bored into mine. I stared back at this sweating madman. Perspiration ran down in rivulets between my breasts, down my stomach, and between my legs. Sweat soaked my jeans and shirt from the sweltering heat. Who was this terrorist and why did he threaten to kill me? At this point I did not know they had killed twenty-four people in the Telaviv hijacking and how ruthless they were.

"Don't look at me, eyes down." He yelled.

Perhaps I should give you the background before you continue reading my frightening story.

In the spring of 1977 Walter Karabian and I were married. We were in love. Walter, who I fondly called Wally, was the youngest man elected to the California Legislature. As the whip for Willy Brown, the Democratic leader of California, Wally was my lawyer and lover. After being a widow for five years I fell in love. We shared a sense of adventure and travel.

Visiting Beirut, Lebanon in 1975 and again in 1977 I felt as if I slipped into a time warp, experiencing another world. The streets were filled with old, dirty Mercedes Benz taxicabs. The odometers clocked over one hundred and thirty thousand miles. Wally and I thought it was peculiar how everyone drove old Mercedes cars that still worked while in Los Angeles, Mercedes were only a luxury car. Walking through the dusty bazaars, we enjoyed the assortment of scents from the different spices, strange fruits, and exotic food. Hypnotizing the tourists the rich markets seemed to distract us from the tensions below the surface. To call it simply, a Middle East political smoke and mirrors. The gold markets lined the main street with Christian-Armenian names on the stores filled with jewelry, fabulous fabrics, and carpets. Wally enjoyed bargaining with them and drinking their coffee.

The bazaars looked like garage sales peddling the same objects. I was happy to explore and eat their amazing food. Everywhere we went the Armenians were delighted to share stories of their lives. They told us that Beirut was the Paris of the Middle East. I knew this was a big stretch from the truth. I spent many fabulous times in Paris, but I restrained from contradicting them, knowing it was not anything like Paris.

The nights in Beirut were fantastic watching the black limousines drive up to our hotel. Arab men in suits wearing colored head scarves flooded the lobby. Women arrived in black burqas and later revealed their exquisite gowns and jewelry. The casino was full of men. The shows were as excellent as the Las Vegas shows. What impressed me the most was the hotel bellboys knew at least five different languages.

Our visit to beautiful Beirut was saddened at the sight of Palestinian ghettos in the city center where people were confined behind twelve-foot fences and unable to leave from dusk to dawn. It was said the ghetto had no plumbing. I knew there would be trouble because you cannot keep people caged like animals for long. After we had left Beirut, a month later there was a riot, and the Civil War broke out that almost devastated Lebanon.

We spent a delightful time in Damascus, Syria where we visited a mosque, learned about their history and ate humungous spreads of food called mezze.

Wally and I attended a meeting of the Ministers of Health with other respected physicians. They were deliberating on how to stop the spread of cholera. They wanted to know how Americans controlled diseases. As they discussed this problem of how to control cholera, one Minister asked for water for everyone. A woman brought in one large pitcher of water, and one glass for the entire group to use.

Wally and I looked at each other knowing at the same time thinking, "There is no hope for this mentality."

That evening leaving the city of Damascus the dark two-lane highway felt foreboding. Looking out the car's window, I saw lights flickering in the small one-room square homes a half a block from the highway. There were no inside bathrooms and the sanitation was far less than what we experience in the western world.

The families gathered on the porch, sitting on the floor they ate together using their hands. Shadows cast on the walls from the one kerosene lantern placed in the middle of the circle of people gave me a feeling of sorrow. These poor people were living in squalor. Most of their population didn't know what a pillow was. I thought if this is the oldest city in the world, why haven't they advanced more?

The Syrian people's extreme poverty gave me such a feeling of gratitude for living in America. I remember being in Syria and looking out across the border to the green fields of Israel, such a contrast. In the same desert one flourishes and the other dies.

Wally and I took our belated honeymoon around the world with John and Agnes Gabriel, both Armenian-Americans. We traveled to Italy, Israel, Syria, Egypt, Russia, and Armenia. John and Wally mainly wanted to visit Armenia. John had relatives there and he made a generous donation to the Armenian Church. Upon arrival, the Armenian Pope greeted us with open arms, permitting us to see the treasures of their church including the cherished display of the Armenian language written in diamonds. It was such an honor to see this in person as I studied their alphabet in preparation of this imminent trip.

I studied Armenian culture and language at UCLA. Being a professional singer, I learned several songs in the Armenian language. I was thrilled to have been granted the privilege to sing for their Pope, the Catholicos. It was the Pope's birthday, and he loved that I sang in English to him. He clapped his hands with joy. "I have never had anyone sing Happy Birthday to me." He said.

I wanted to learn their language to communicate with the people in Armenian. My vocabulary wasn't extensive but I could understand the most elementary of conversations. When I sang, "The Lord's Prayer," in their language and different music, the Pope clapped his hands. He said he wanted to give me a new Armenian name. He named me, Vartanique, which meant small pink rose. I was honored and adored the kind Armenians. It humbled me to see how little most of these people had just to survive, yet they generously shared with us their delicious food and offered great hospitality.

Another thing I noticed was the fact that their street signs were in Armenian, not Russian like the other dominated countries of the Soviet Union.

The man I married was American. While visiting Armenia and spending time there, I was able to witness firsthand how women waited on their husband's hand and foot. They even stood behind their spouse's chairs waiting for them to finish their meals before they ate. When we returned home, Wally became more Armenian in his actions towards me, forgetting he had married a successful, independent, American woman! His disrespect and constant unfaithfulness ruined our marriage.

Arriving in Egypt was a relief after being in Russia. I never felt safe in Russia with men spying on us and following us everywhere. I was happy to be in a friendly country. It was disconcerting to see men sleeping everywhere on the floor in the airport. I had to step over them in my high heels just to get to the baggage claim area!

As we drove to our hotel, I watched old men in long white caftans sweeping the streets with handmade brooms. I felt sorry for them and wondered why the government didn't give them proper machines to keep their highways clean.

After we checked into our hotel I took a swim in the cool pool. The water felt wonderful after the long flight and hot drive. I heard giggling and observed several teenage boys peeking at me through the bushes. They were relieving themselves sexually. Disgusted, I left the pool and rested in my room before our next few days of sightseeing.

That evening we took a night sail on the River Nile. I couldn't believe I was sailing on the river that I had read all my life in the Bible. Our friends John and Agnes Gabriel requested that I sing a few songs. It seemed incongruous to sing modern melodies in this antique setting. A peace surrounded us sailing on the dark river.

After several days of walking in the pyramids in the Valley of the Kings, Wally and I decided that we had enough climbing down empty tombs. We enjoyed the impressive Cairo museum with most of King Tutankhamun's treasures. We giggled how disrespectful many of the mummies were left on the floor. I almost tripped on one and saw the toes broken off on several of them.

On the way to our hotel we stopped at the shops where we spotted a tall wooden vase designed with mother of pearl hieroglyphics. It was fun watching Wally negotiate a better price with the shop owners that lasted nearly two hours and lots of coffee and cigars.

September 27th, 1977, we drove to the airport and continued our journey to Bangkok on an all-night flight. I decided to stay comfortable and casual for my travels since no one was meeting us at the airport. I wore jeans and tennis shoes. I usually wore a dress and heels, but I didn't want to step over the sleeping bodies again in high heels at the filthy Egyptian airport.

We boarded the Douglas DC-8 Japanese Air Lines Flight 472. The flight originated in Paris and was scheduled to land in Athens, Cairo, Karachi, Bombay, and then on to Bangkok. Later, the plane was expected to fly to Haneda Airport in Tokyo with 14 crew on board and 156 passengers.

We flew all night high above Kuwait and the Arab Emirates. Pressing my face against the window, I watched the fires burning from the hundreds of oil wells. The rush of anticipation tingled through me seeing this strange part of the world. We refueled in Pakistan in the early morning hours. Being excited to be on the other side of the world kept me awake. I couldn't wait to visit Pakistan. I got off the plane in Karachi to look around the airport.

Everything displayed was unusual, even the spicy, pungent smells. A keenness intensified in me knowing I was visiting a weird and wonderful part of the world that few Americans had the opportunity to visit. I was amused by strange objects offered for sale at the airport shops. I purchased a small hand-made woodwind as I collected unusual musical instruments on my world travels.

We arrived in Bombay, India at dawn. My legs needed to stretch, so I walked outside the first-class section and stood on the top of the stair's platform. Feeling the exhaustion from no sleep, the smell of gasoline fumes nauseated me.

I turned back inside the cabin where I observed men in blue uniforms arguing with men in black suits. They were comparing their lists. I felt uneasy

I later learned the multinational passengers were from the USA, Egypt, India, Pakistan, Saudi Arabia, Kenya, Greece, Jordan, Korea and the Philippines. I watched people board and the stewardesses carried on board little waxy boxes that looked like lunch boxes. They dropped them on the couch in first class. Then, after putting their personal things away, they casually threw the yellow boxes in the overhead bins. I sat in the front seat of first class and was able to see each person as they boarded. Several Japanese men were dressed like crew and carried black bags.

CHAPTER TWO

# TERROR
# IN THE SKIES

**T**he plane took off at 6 a.m. in the morning from Bombay. The stewardess announced breakfast would be served in forty minutes. I was sleepy, so I untied my tennis shoes, slipped them off and unfastened my brassiere under my shirt. I closed my eyes content that I could sleep for a little while.

About twenty minutes later, maybe 75 kilometers out of Bombay I was awakened by screaming and yelling in the back of the plane. Several men, clad in black with faces covered in red and white checkered scarves shouted orders. They ran up the aisle carrying guns and hand grenades yelling, "Sit, sit, passports, sit. Hands up!" They moved quickly and confiscated everyone's passports, pens, and identification. I think I went into shock since I couldn't believe it was happening for the first several minutes.

17

Some passengers stood up to get their travel documents from the overhead bins and were forcibly pistol-whipped down. People fell to the floor from being hit by the butt of the guns, screaming and bleeding.

"SIT! SIT! DON'T LOOK AT ME!" commanded the men with covered heads and faces. Several people were knocked out. One man fell right in the aisle by my side and didn't move for many hours. I thought he was dead.

"HANDS UP! UP, UP, IN THE AIR," they commanded.

I heard a baby crying in the back of the plane. The commotion grew louder. One of the terrorists yelled back, "SHUT UP, SHUT UP, SHUT UP!" The fanatic kept yelling, "Stop crying, shut up, shut up!" The baby cried louder. I was terrified he would kill the child.

The passengers could not understand their broken English as the terrorists shouted their commands. They wanted our passports, but they didn't want us to stand up to get them from the overhead bins. They pushed the purser and stewardess down and made them sit in the seats belted. They roared, "SEAT BELTS. SEAT BELTS!"

Two of the terrorists shook like leaves in the wind and waved their guns at us. One was smaller than the rest of them. He was always blowing his nose. I could see the sweat running down his nose and lips, his scarf soaked with perspiration. Their movements were quick like they were young men. Terrified a weapon would go off, and the plane would go down, the passengers complied. These were the most horrifying moments on the aircraft. The plane made several sharp turns.

Each hijacker held in one hand a cocked pistol and carried a hand grenade in the other with a thumb or index finger through the pin of the grenade. They kept their guns pointed at us. The first few hours they were aggressive and very tense. They were always looking from side to side keeping an eye on everyone.

My husband's hazel eyes looked peculiar as he whispered, "This is the real thing. If we don't get killed on the plane, it will be a miracle." He too was worried a gun would go off with our plane in the air.

Our friends, John and Agnes Gabriel traveled with us and I hoped they were not too frightened. Agnes sat still and calm, while her husband, John was squirming in his seat. He, a wealthy, influential Armenian banker from East Los Angeles, certainly did not take orders well! Agnes kept him calm by holding his hand, whispering, "Hush, hush, don't talk."

After an hour of sheer intimidation, each passenger willingly gave up their travel documents and followed directions without question. The hijackers required the stewardesses to stay belted in their seats. The rest of the passengers were instructed to keep their arms and hands above their heads like in the prison camps. My stomach quivered feeling the anxiety. Wally and I tried to whisper to comfort each other and touched each other's elbows to keep close.

I kept thinking this wasn't really happening, but the longer we kept our arms raised high it became clearer that we were trapped in prison 35 thousand feet high in the air. For hours we weren't allowed to move. The itchy numbness spread from my fingers to the rest of my body. It seemed surreal as if I were watching this event but not a part of it. It felt like I was in a movie or a nightmare from which I couldn't awake. I couldn't believe it was happening to us.

It is odd how I reacted to this traumatic situation. I thought strange things like, "Here I am without my shoes or bra done up, I'll have to walk all over India without shoes. We will be killed somewhere over India, and no one will find us!"

With my trembling hands high in the air I realized my long red nails might bring attention to my diamond ring. Terrified someone would see me I waited until no hijacker was looking, I slipped my ring off my finger and put it inside my brassiere. Seeing this, my husband whispered, "Good for you."

It was such an automatic act that I didn't think about it. It was a reflex that later seemed silly. I would have given everything I had just to be free!

After taking control of the airplane, the hijackers entered the cockpit grabbed the intercom away from the pilot and announced, "We are the Japanese Red Army."

Wally and I looked at each other wondering who was the Japanese Red Army, the JRA? We had never heard of them.

I could hear the JAL pilot trying to get clearance to land in several nearby airports, but none would allow them to land. Our plane had circled two other airports for almost three hours. The Indian government wouldn't allow them to land in their country. They even blocked the runways with trucks not to let them land and chased them away with their fighter jets. What seemed endless we flew another hour or more when I heard yelling in the cockpit. Our pilot said, "Dacca, we are out of fuel, we are coming down.

The response was, "No, no. Do not land! We have aircraft leaving."

The plane answered, "We are coming down! WE ARE OUT OF FUEL!"

Again, Dacca's response was, "No, no you cannot land. We have too many flights leaving. Don't land!"

The plane jerked left then right. I saw a jet fly right past us almost hitting our flight. Another aircraft leaving the Dacca airport flew so close to us that our plane shuddered. I thought it was going to crash into us and we would die. After circling overhead Dacca for a few more minutes, the plane abruptly swerved descending as the tower ordered the pilots not to land. Almost losing the contents of my stomach, the plane touched down without permission. Everyone sighed from relief. I heard yelling from the tower, ordering where to park the aircraft. Disobeying their orders, I was inquisitive to see where we were. I raised the window shades slightly.

21

Peeking out the sliver of the window I noted a thick jungle at the end of the runway.

# CHAPTER THREE

# ON THE GROUND

**T**he silence was ominous and foreboding as we waited. No one moved or said anything. I prayed, thankful that we were safely on the ground and alive! Several hours passed, and there was still no movement. No vehicles came to our plane. Not one person came close to our aircraft. It was as if we weren't there or a force prevented any contact from the outside world. We sat in our seats petrified. The hijackers didn't contact the tower for another three hours. They barely spoke to each other and called each other by numbers. They were very organized and well trained. I watched them go about their business in the front galley unwinding plastic explosives. They threaded the explosives down the plane's aisles on both sides and around each seat. My heart thumped trying to think of ways to stop them.

Flying through the night and sitting on the plane all day my back cramped, my neck and legs ached. I could feel the heat rising making me dizzy. I felt drained, nauseous, dehydrated. My mouth bone dry, I needed a drink of water. By evening, the terrorists told us we could put our arms down, but we had to keep our hands clasped in our laps. My head throbbed from a migraine headache, and my arms limp from being raised so long. I kept thinking, "Who are these fanatics and what do they want?"

Being a couple of months pregnant I had to go to the bathroom. Everything hurt in my body. The temperature grew hotter and hotter. Perspiration dripped down my face; little rivulets ran down my breasts and stomach. My wet shirt and jeans clung to me. My body ached. Everything seemed to be moving in an alternative reality. I almost fainted. I knew these crazy men were now in control of my life.

The airplane sat on the ground for four hours with no communication. The wait was hideous. Finally, the hijackers communicated with the tower. I heard them announce, "This is the Japanese Red Army speaking; To the Japanese people and the people over the world, we announce Japan Flight JAL 472, has been taken over by the Hidaka Commando Unit of the Japanese Red Army."

The Bangladesh tower replied: "This is Dhaka tower." The Japanese Ambassador, Ichiro Yashioka was introduced to the hijackers.

The terrorist answered in broken English: "We will call ourselves Danke. Now we are preparing execution. You tell

Japanese government if Japanese government does not agree to our demands they will take full responsibility for the execution of the passengers. We are choosing passengers one by one. We will execute passengers every three hours. First one will be an American Jew, John Gabriel. We are ready to take next action."

Being in the First-Class front seat I could hear most of the conversation between the tower and the plane.

Hours later General Zia, the President of Bangladesh appointed his Air Vice Marshall A.G. Mahmud to oversee the negotiations. When Mahmud spoke to the terrorist he was incredibly polite. Slowly Mahmud repeated several times what the hijackers said and what they wanted.

"This is control tower. I've got your message. I've told you earlier that the problem can be solved. We are trying to find a solution. I have no doubt that a solution will come. I also request that you not embarrass Bangladesh government. We have made all efforts to solve your problem. I can assure you things can be resolved without your action. Your problem can be solved giving some patience and time without taking this action. Please confirm what I said."

The leader of the Japanese Red Army replied in his broken English: "We appreciate your effort to solve this problem, and you tried your best. We appreciate, but we have waited enough already. We waited very much time. The Japanese government is trying to lose time. This is their way. We know that. We have enough years fighting against Japanese regime. We know their tricks and their behavior. We cannot wait for more. Now we will carry out action, according to our plan. Anyway, we call you at 5 p.m. before executing one of the passengers."

Knowing that John Gabriel had been picked to be the first one killed left me full of dread. The hijackers must have thought John Gabriel was Jewish since he was an American banker and had on a large diamond ring. The JRA were wrong assuming he was a Jew. John was Armenian, Christian.

After 4 p.m. I heard the pilot request fuel. The hijackers gave lengthy statements against the Japanese government. They demanded six million dollars in one hundred American dollar bills and twelve of their comrades to be released from Japanese prisons and brought to Dacca.

JRA: "In respect, we have discussed with our unit, and we have reached a conclusion. We cannot release all passengers. It is impossible because our first principle is we must guarantee to protect the aircraft and lives of the crew and ourselves. Remember why we landed here? We thought the Bangladesh government is an independent Islamic and popular government. We believed that you could help us, and you can be a representative of the regime between the Japanese and us."

The long hours of no response from the tower continued when finally, the Japanese Ambassador, Ichiro Yashioka tried to explain to the hijackers how the demands would take more time. Air Vice Marshall Mahmud needed to consult the Japanese government to see if they would comply with the requests.

Our captor grew impatient. He yelled, "I kill one person every three hours until our demands are met." Then the leader, Osamu Maruoka left the cockpit and walked down the aisle of the first-class section studying all of us. His menacing look frightened me. I could feel panic starting to surface, so I kept on silently calling to Jesus to keep me calm and repeating the Lord's Prayer.

The terrorist leader stared at each of us one by one. His frustration made him more dangerous. After checking us out in the first-class section, he entered the cockpit again and announced fuming to the tower, "The first to be killed is John Gabriel, the Jewish American banker. If our demands are not met, we will kill John Gabriel at 12:00 noon the next day."

I shuddered and almost let out a scream! I was hoping John hadn't heard the bad news. My mind couldn't accept what was happening. Who were these wild men waving their guns in our faces?

I had never heard of the Japanese Red Army, who I later discovered has trained with the Palestine Liberation Organization, known as the PLO. No wonder they labeled John as a Jew to be killed first! They had committed horrific terrorism a few years earlier, but in retrospect I was grateful I didn't know this at the time.

I tried thinking how can I protect myself? Why did no one fight them? Who were these madmen? Why did they wear such hot scarves for masks? They were profusely sweating and acted like they were high on drugs.

The hijackers looked Japanese. I was told later the leader's name was Osamu Maruoka. Being a notorious terrorist, he didn't need to hide his face. He told the tower, "We are Freedom Fighters from the Japanese Red Army. We have demands."

No one contacted the tower again. There was an eerie silence. I didn't know who these hijackers were and what they wanted. For several more hours, the radio was silent. The hijackers paced the aisles closing the window shades and checking people's pockets, taking pens, keys, and passports. Each saboteur knew his job. They quickly started unwinding plastic explosives and laying them down the aisles so that at any moment they would be ready to blow up the plane.

They yelled at the passengers, "Sit, sit, hands up, don't look at me, eyes down, no getting up. Keep still, no standing up." If anyone stood up, they were pistol-whipped.

I had never seen men fall into submission so fast as I saw my husband and the other men around me in the first-class section. They meekly lowered their eyes and were silent.

§

"My Lord," I thought, "I've trained tougher horses who fought harder for their freedom than anyone on this plane." The memory of spending time as a child with my father's racehorses helped keep away reality. I remembered spending Sundays together with my mother, father, two brothers, and three sisters. My parents always insisted Sundays were for our family to be together. Every Sunday after church service, Dad took us out for Sunday dinner at one of his favorite restaurants. Dad drove us to Northridge Farms for the afternoon to check on our racehorses. He let us name the little ones. It was always a pleasurable time naming and watching the colts run and play. Dad would take me to the races on Saturdays, and I grew up loving being with our horses.

§

Happy for a few moments recalling my childhood, loud shouting in the back of the plane ripped me back to the present. The guns and hand grenades were intimidating. My mind raced. I wouldn't accept this as my fate. I kept thinking of ways to escape. I remembered I had a pen in my jeans . . . Could I poke out an eye with it? Could I knock out a gun from their hands? Would anyone help me? It was odd to see human beings reduced to such an impassive state with no free will.

The hijackers wouldn't listen to anyone on the plane including the purser whose name was Tecasey Ikesue. Tecasey tried to assure them that everyone would cooperate. He stood up to talk, and one of the terrorists cracked him over the head with a pistol. Blood ran. He fell back as the blood poured on his white uniform.

I tried to memorize what weapon each hijacker carried. Wally, familiar with guns, could identify them with a cursory glance. They had a loaded automatic pistol, 32 caliber pistols; one Lava, Barrette, Star and an Argentine gun. They wore gloves and always had their fingers on the triggers. They knew what to do and their chain of command was evident. There was a captain, a lieutenant, and three soldiers. The three soldiers patrolled the cabins; the lieutenant stayed at the front, and the captain was in the cockpit. They spoke in Japanese and Arabic. Later they were more open about speaking Arabic with Arab speaking passengers. They hardly spoke English.

Their red and white material around their heads resembled what the Palestinians wore in the Middle East back in 1975 when I visited Lebanon and Syria. Their head scarves only revealed a small opening for their eyes.

"Don't look at me, lower your eyes!" The kidnappers shouted.

Frustration stabbed my insides like a swarm of angry hornets stinging my nerves. I kept asking myself, what can I do to stop them? No one could move or leave their seats. If they did, the hijackers hit the passengers' heads with their guns. Their leader took charge. Most passengers had boarded in Cairo, except for a large group of Japanese tourists returning from Europe.

§

I later learned there were no metal detectors in Cairo or any of the other major airports. The Japanese terrorists disguised the guns in their "crew luggage."

§

Six hours after the plane landed in Dacca, the hot, air-less temperature rose horribly. The passengers couldn't stand the heat. The Arab travelers were the most affected by the debilitating 120 degrees. The arms of the seats had little metal ashtrays on the top of them where one's arms rested. The metal was so scorching that I could not place my forearms on them when the hijackers finally let us put our arms down. Feeling agony in my back and shoulders, I tried to turn in my seat to find a comfortable position to sleep. Impossible!

The stench from the passenger's perspiration overwhelmed me. I tried breathing through my mouth to arrest the putrid smells to no avail. My body was losing fluids. I wondered how much moisture a body can lose without replenishing it. I desperately needed water! My stomach growled from no food or water. Feeling the anguish, I visualized being under a cold waterfall and practiced my meditation in the hopes of forgetting for a few minutes the distress I was experiencing. My hands still shaking, I felt like I would vomit.

I figured I was six to eight weeks pregnant. Wally and I had married in May but waited until September to take our "around the world" honeymoon, so my young boys could acclimate to the new school year and home. We were both excited to welcome a new life into the world, but the stress from knowing I had a little one growing inside me made me feel even worse. I knew this sizzling heat could hurt my baby. A strong feeling of urgency rushed over me. I had been without food and water for over 16 hours and felt sick. I was hungry and dehydrated. I was petrified from fear and felt dizzy and fragile. With each breath the blistering heat felt like I was suffocating. I needed water.

I studied the hijacker who was guarding our first-class section. With his face still wrapped in a red and white checkered scarf, he breathed heavily and sweltered like the rest of us from the heat. Standing most of the time, his small hands quivered. He tried to cover his excitement by moving them and constantly blowing his nose! Yet, I always felt his eyes watching me.

The pungent stench of the toilets and the sweltering tropical heat almost drove me delirious! Trapped, not knowing how to handle my pain, I focused my mind on something else by singing to myself Puccini's arias, "*O Mio Babbino Caro.*" I sang this song to my boys many times to put them to sleep. It helped distract my attention from my discomfort. Music has always soothed my soul. As the music played in my head, it gave me a sense of relief. Music always filled in the cracks of uncertainty for me.

My sister and I studied piano at USC when I was six. I distracted myself by playing the piano keys in the air. Remembering the opera arias I had sung in concerts, I silently sang Puccini's La Boheme in my head. To ease my fear I silently sang the words in different languages but when I imagined an English song I cried.

Would I ever sing to my boys again? Remembering their faces, I wondered what they might be doing at home. I was frightened that I would never be with them again. My tears fell, but the combination of perspiration and tears looked and felt the same.

I don't know why I was steadfast for these young radicals not to see me fragile. Perhaps being a proud American gave me that determination. I wondered what kind of tragedies drove these young men to risk their lives and be so cruel. I thanked

God for my blessed life compared to the unhappiness they must be living. I tried to feel sorry for them, but all I could think about was finding a way to stop them! Something inside me snapped, and I knew I would never be the same again.

Their captain, Maruoka, walked like a crazed animal past me. His presence frightened me. I kept my eyes down until he passed me, then I concentrated looking at his aura above his head. It was dangerously brown and black. Instead of being rounded like a halo, it was jagged and spiked. I felt he was pure evil. I silently called to Jesus Christ to save me and protect me from his menacing looks.

At 8 p.m., Maruoka asked for an air conditioner truck. An airport security officer, Okuba, set up the air conditioner. He was the only man permitted to speak to one of the terrorists who was an engineer. He told him how to set up the air conditioner. I could see that he and the co-pilot communicated with the security officer by hand signs. He finished and left, but the air conditioning was not functioning.

I prayed all night long asking for God's protection. I made many promises to Christ if he saved me. Tears ran down my cheeks as I thought of my two little boys and fought to visualize us home together. I remembered the Dali Lama said if we visualize something a thousand times it will be manifested. I kept seeing my boys laughing on my bed reading the Sunday newspaper comics. I found myself in this safe place in my mind for a short time, but the static and piercing yelling from the terrorists ripped me back to this desperate situation.

Still, there was no request or conversation from the tower. Hours after we landed, the Japanese Red Army hijackers finally proposed their request. The leader started giving his demands and yelling, "We demand twelve of our comrades taken out of jail and six million American one hundred-dollar bills brought here to Dacca. We kill one American every three hours if you don't meet our demands." Hearing his menacing words made me want to wretch.

I heard Air Vice Marshall A.G. Mahmud patiently trying to explain that it will take a lot of time, days to find each of the prisoners and get their release. He tried to tell them that their requests had to be agreed on by the Japanese Government, who they contacted immediately.

Three hijackers patrolled the rows watching us. I found myself wanting to be invisible. When I saw a terrorist turn his back, I quickly braided my long blond hair and tucked it in at the back of my neck. Sweat dripped off my face, so there were no remnants of my makeup, a closer step to blending in and being invisible among the others.

John and Agnes Gabriel were elderly; with prostrate problems, John squirmed in his seat, and I could see his discomfort. If he went too long dehydrated, he would be critically ill. After several hours of not being told anything, not allowed to go to the bathroom, not allowed to drink water, not allowed to eat, I decided to help John Gabriel who I fondly called "Papa." I couldn't just sit there and watch him suffer. I wanted to comfort John and Agnes.

# CHAPTER FOUR

# GUN IN MY MOUTH

**T**he situation was getting worse and instead of being fearful, I felt protective of John Gabriel and decided to help him. I looked around to see if anyone was watching me. The terrorists were engaged in the front lounge section and were not watching us. I unbuckled my seatbelt, slipped on my tennis shoes and fastened my brassiere. Looking again to be sure no one was near me, I cautiously moved out of my seat. Holding my hands in the air, high above my head, stepping delicately over explosives, I felt as if I were moving in slow motion. I tiptoed down the aisle knowing it was a minefield. The temperature had now reached well over 120 degrees. Some passengers watched me with dread and others acted like I was invisible. They had a look of hopelessness and almost a disconnection of what was going on. Quickly I disappeared into the bathroom. After relieving a long overdue full bladder, I rinsed my face and neck.

Disobeying the hijackers to get water for John or my "Papa" as I called him was natural for me. John gave me away at my wedding. I loved him like a father. My natural propensity was to help a loved one. I thought, "What can they do, shoot me? That will be fast: I might not feel it for a minute, then die. That's OK, but what if I tripped on the explosive under my feet or a hand grenade? What if it severed me into pieces and I didn't die? What if I caused a sudden explosion killing everyone?" The worst image was seeing my arms blown off or legs severed and the pain of surviving as a disabled person. My heart pounded. I wasn't thinking but acting more from instinct. All of us felt the degrading heat and were desperately thirsty.

Determined not to be intimidated by my fears, I juggled five small white paper cups back to the front of the plane. Stepping over the explosives, I negotiated back to John's seat trying not to spill the water. John drank two tiny cups and passed the three paper cups to the others in the first class. Each person took a small sip saving for the next person in a beautiful act of kindness.

I heard the terrorist say to the tower… "We kill Americans first every three hours!" Everyone was studying me, and I felt exposed. I sensed the eyes of the leader observing my actions helping John. He moved from his position and jerked the back of my head by my hair shoving a gun in my mouth. I gritted my teeth trying to keep my lips closed, but the metal pushed hard against my teeth hurting my lips and gums.

I looked deeply into his eyes and saw the depth of evil and the devil in his soul. We stared at each other for what felt like an eternity. I could taste blood in my mouth, but I didn't stop staring back into his eyes. I felt like yelling, "Shoot me you Bastard, you slimy weakling. I dare you, shoot me!"

"Don't look at me! This is no joke. This is serious business!" He growled at me pushing the gun harder into my mouth. "Don't get up again. I'LL KILL YOU!"

He pushed me back into my seat. My mouth hurt. It felt like the nozzle of the gun was still pressing against my gums. I tried touching my tongue against my teeth to relieve the pain. He hurt me! My head was woozy, but I wouldn't let him see me injured. My heart knocked against my ribcage. I felt like everyone could hear it. Not moving I watched him, and he walked back to the cockpit shouting again at the negotiating team in the tower.

Being an American proud of our freedoms, I seethed knowing this misguided, horrible creature would dare put a gun in my mouth. How dare he do this to me! Until it happens, one cannot fathom the fight of wits trying not to show fear to these cowards and being demeaned as a human being. My honor was assaulted, and I wanted to kill this wild animal!

I heard the leader demanding six million American dollars in one hundred bills, not Japanese currency. I heard Mahmud's soft voice trying to calm the agitated hijackers. "I spoke to you on this subject very logically. We both are working to analyze that position. I understand you want some shared understanding or some identity of trust. I agree that it is necessary for me and of course for you to have evidence of this subject. But we will not agree to give you any of your comrades until the passengers are released."

The passengers had no idea if the Japanese government would try to find their comrades in jail, which would take more time. No one told us if the government was trying to obtain the money. We knew nothing except what I heard from the cockpit.

He yelled louder, "We kill one American every three hours if you do not meet our demands. We kill Americans first every three hours!" He continued making announcements over the intercom. He said again to the hostages on the plane that the airplane had been taken over by the Hidaka of the Japanese Red Army, whoever they were!

§

It was a blessing that I did not know the severity of the situation or for what the JRA stood. I later found out that they were the most hardened terrorists at that time. I learned the JRA was so vicious that in the early 70s they took 14 of their own members, tortured them for 3 days without food nor water, and left them on crosses in the ocean to die. If they did not drown, they were innocent. If they drowned, they were guilty. All of them drowned. Additionally, it was later revealed to me that the JRA was responsible for the massacre at the LOD Airport (Ben Gurion) in May 1972.

They arrived carrying violin cases with Kalashnikov assault rifles with stocks removed and grenades. When they arrived at the Japan Airlines area, they started shooting and tossing hand grenades. They massacred 17 Puerto Rican pilgrims and 7 Israelis. Now members who shared the same mentality and affinity toward violence held me, my husband, my friends, and other passengers hostage on this plane.

*CHAPTER FIVE*

# FEARFUL NIGHT

The terrorists separated couples and put my husband across the aisle. We were told to keep our hands up in the air. Everyone was looking down and cowering in their seats. A Saudi Arabian man was hit in the head because he looked up at them.

Some passengers tried to relieve themselves from the heat. Arab male passengers took off their clothes and only kept on their underwear. The hijackers were also perspiring but kept on their clothes and scarves that covered their faces. One terrorist acted like he couldn't breathe. I called him the Sniffer because he cut a hole in his mask around his mouth to blow his nose all the time. He was the bomb expert and had a familiarity with the airplane. Sniffer must have been an airline employee since he knew the aircraft better than the others. He had a blue binder that showed an airline guide: how to operate things, for instance how to operate the stove, heat the water, etc.

All night I heard them in the cockpit giving deadlines. They said they were going to kill us at 9:00 p.m., at 12 midnight then again at 3:00a.m. if their demands were not met. I would whisper to the others what they were telling the tower. Since we couldn't talk to each other, we started a sign language communication. I kept trying to devise a plan to protect myself and maybe even kill one of them. It amazed me being such a loving Christian woman I could conceive killing someone. Everything changes when you are in a life-threatening situation. My life took on a whole new perspective. Just thinking about killing him gave me a sickening feeling all through my body. I started to shake and became short of breath. This was dangerously real; it wasn't a movie or television show. This was revolting and intimidating terror. I believed they would kill me.

I watched the smaller, thin hijacker guarding us. When he turned his body away from me, I observed another gun in his back belt. I thought about pulling out his gun and shooting him before he turned around. I hesitated because my experience with automatic guns was the knowledge the guns sometimes jammed.

I also had the idea of strangling the puny terrorist with the earphones left around our seats. Having moved Wally away, they sat a stranger next to me. The American had his two gold Cross pins in his shirt pocket, and I whispered to him, "You can poke out his eyes with your pens." I went through step-by-step things with him how we could defend ourselves. I couldn't convince him! It took me hours to get him to agree to help me if I tried to get the little one. My husband had a pocketknife with a small 2-inch blade. I knew Wally could cut one's throat, but the biggest question that plagued us was where do you stick the knife? Do you stick it on the side or the front? Do you cut the windpipe or the jugular vein on the side? We didn't know if that would stop a person from screaming by cutting the front part of the throat. I couldn't believe I was remembering these things and planning how to kill someone.

Reality shot through me as the small hijacker brushed by me acting like he was on cocaine or something that made his nose run all the time. He fidgeted dangling his gun in my direction. It scared me that it was pointed at me most of the time.

I couldn't believe my body could lose so much moisture from perspiration. Sweat dripped from my hair. My clothes, completely drenched, clung to me. No relief. To distract myself from the stifling heat I visualized being on Kauai in Hawaii many years ago before with my first husband Larry Doheny. We went swimming in the cold water pool under the twin waterfalls. This was a magical place touched by delicate scents of tropical flowers.

I was jerked back to the present by the shrill screams of the hijacker. He was shouting into the phone commanding the tower again. The longer Murouka waited for a reply, the more violent his voice became. People around me in first class stayed very calm and silent. I was amazed how quickly a weapon puts one in power of so many.

The hijackers opened the plane's door for a short time for air. The unbearable heat brought several Arab men from the back section forward. Some of the Sudanese and Egyptian men came forward looking like zombies. They had on no clothing except a small cloth covering their privates. Their naked dripping bodies kept walking forward, gasping, begging for air. The eight men pressed forward into our cabin. I kept thinking why don't they just push the hijackers out the door? Then others came forward begging for cigarettes. "Cigarette. Cigarette," they pleaded.

How ridiculous their actions seemed to me. Without water, food, and barely allowed to go to the toilet, the Arabs wanted to smoke! The terrorist closed the door thinking a sniper might shoot them. Two hijackers then pointed their guns and herded the passengers back down the aisle to their seats. That was one of the strangest things I had ever seen.

Whenever one of the hijackers came down the aisle, Wally motioned that I was pregnant by moving his arms like I had a baby and pointing to my stomach. He did that every time until he could to be confident they understood him. Eventually one of the hijackers acknowledged his movements.

Feeling vulnerable I wanted to communicate with Wally but the hijackers moved him to the back of the plane. The lights were turned off. It was dark except for the dim lights over the toilets. I watched two hijackers resting in the front lounge while two others stood guard. I felt weak and defenseless.

I never thought I would be in this situation, helpless and crying inside for my little boys. My back hurt, my arms hurt, my legs hurt, everything hurt, and were cramping from the long flights with no movement.

I wondered if I died, who would take care of my boys? Probably Larry Doheny's cousins, their godparents, Linda and Michael Niven, would take them. I could see my little boy's beautiful faces laughing, smiling, and hugging me. I prayed to Jesus to let us go home safely and be a family together again. I visualized being with them playing in our backyard. I wondered if they knew how terrified I felt at the thought of never seeing my two precious boys again? Would they remember how much I loved them? Would they know they were my entire life? How would they grow up without a father and a mother? A wave of extreme dread made me nauseous. Dry heaves attacked me. There was no food in me, so it was just the reaction from nerves and being pregnant.

Exhaustion exposed my raw nerves. I was unable to control my emotions. I couldn't stop feeling powerless. I didn't show my anxiety but looking around at all the passengers, just sitting still waiting to be slaughtered like defenseless cattle, made me sick. Why don't they fight back? I only had one person who I knew would help me, my husband. Perhaps I could try to overcome one of the terrorists. I wish I knew Martial Arts. I wish I had a gun. I wish I were home safely with my children. Tears rolled down my face even more as I felt a mother's deep love for her boys. Strange, I didn't think about being a film star, my family, or any of my friends. I could only see the faces of my two precious boys.

I pretended I was talking to them and telling them a story of this experience. My sons Sean and Ryan were so young, how could they understand? I couldn't even fathom why this was happening. I tried to stay in that comfort zone remembering good times when the truth shot through me as a hijacker walked by me grunting as he moved down the aisle.

I heard the hijackers' hostility into the phone to the tower. "We want twelve comrades released from jail and brought to Dacca with a plane. We won't release anyone until we get our friends out of jail. If you don't agree to our demands, we kill one person every three hours, Americans first."

Silence ensued from the tower radio when finally, Air Vice Marshall Mahmud repeated several times exactly what the hijacker stipulated. It took several minutes for him to repeat everything and then again repeated the same thing very slowly.

Murouka became agitated and yelled, "Stop taking so long. Tell us if you are meeting our demands."

The longer Murouka waited for a reply, the more violent the leader's voice became. There was no answer for many hours. People around me in first class stayed silent. Some were sleeping. How could they be so calm? Were they as scared as I was?

At midnight, the air-conditioning was turned on. Dripping wet from the heat the cold air made us shiver. I couldn't understand why these crazy men kept the air off in the day but turned it on in the night. The air conditioning made noise, so part of the night I couldn't hear the hijackers talking to the tower.

One terrorist stood right near me and played with his gun. He was fiddling with the bullets taking them out and then putting them back into his weapon over and over. The Lieutenant had a clip in the back belt and held a .32 pistol.

I thought if he shot me, I probably wouldn't feel the bullet at first being in shock. I was familiar with guns. Wally and I hunted quail and pheasants, and I took target practice with a .45 at the Police Academy with Larry. Guns didn't intimidate me, but what terrified me were the explosives on the floor and the hand grenades ready to blow us up. Being dismembered by the grenades was disproportionately the inhibiting feature that made me cautious.

My back hurt and pain shot down my legs from not moving all night and day. My body felt like it would melt away having been rendered weak from all the perspiring. Without water I knew I was not in great shape.

As the hours wore on, the hijackers made a few announcements. Two times they were on the intercom to say something about who they were, but they never gave us information about the negotiations. We didn't know if their government was trying to meet their demands. I heard Air Vice Marshall Mahmud repeat slowly what the hijacker said and it would come through clearly. They spoke in English since it is the universal air language. Mahmud repeated what the hijacker requested slowly and clearly. Sometimes I could hear the hijacker's intensity in his voice grow, and he would yell back at the Air Vice Marshal when he repeated everything several times. The longer Murouka waited for a reply, the more vehement his voice became. The more agitated the leader became, the more I thought they would start killing us sooner as he said they would.

Looking at the first-class passengers so silent and passive confused me. Did they feel like I did or was I the only one who wanted to fight these demons?

Finally, the hijackers started letting people go to the toilets one by one. That was one of the most sickening experiences. After several Arabs went to the bathroom, it became disgusting. The Arabs would defecate, wipe and drop it on the floor instead in the toilet. The stench was repulsive. The kindest act was after an Arab would finish, the Japanese women would go in and clean up their mess the best they could and leave little perfume bottles to help repel the smell. I quickly learned to follow a Japanese woman to the bathroom.

CHAPTER SIX

# FIRST RELEASED

**T**he second day at 8:45 a.m. Marouka told me I was getting off the plane. After two days I was one of the first five to be removed. I thought they were taking me off to shoot me! All night they screamed at the tower, "We kill American every three hours!" I was convinced they would shoot me.

It astonished me when I really believed I would die, how desperately I wanted to live! I couldn't die like this. I knew God had a bigger plan for me than to leave my two fatherless boys without a mother. I believed they would kill me because they were vicious, horrible men. Our lives meant nothing to them, and they had no feeling of remorse for hurting us. I had never seen such evil demonstrated right in front of my eyes. I learned that there really is a devil, and these men were full of the impiety.

If I were being released, part of me felt guilty that others were still left on the plane. As they prepared me to leave, Wally came forward. I looked into my husband's eyes expressing all the significant things one wants the other to know believing I might never see him again. I begged for them to release Wally with me, but the hijacker said: "No, he goes with us until the end of the excursion." I didn't know what that meant.

When it was certain that I was being taken off the plane, passengers started coming up to me or passing their possessions to me in their dirty socks. Arab and Indian men came forward to me and handed me their wedding rings. Other passengers naked except for their underwear held out money and jewelry. These hot frightened men of different religions and backgrounds trusted me with their life treasures for safe keeping. I was given money worth thousands of dollars, notes, jewelry and personal items. And yet, I had no idea if I was going to be shot or released.

If I lived and they didn't, how would I give back their treasures? I stuffed them in my pockets and prayed that I would see them again. It was such an act of a faith on their part that I was reminded God was watching over us and there might be a satisfactory ending after all.

An Indian couple with a little girl, Mr. and Mrs. George Verghese, lived in Glendora, California told the hijackers he and his wife had visited India for the past month and she was recovering from cholera. The terrorists freaked out demanding liquor to wash their hands and where they sat. An American man fell on the floor near me. He didn't move for the whole day and night. He said he was recovering also from cholera. Apparently, there had been a breakout recently of this disease in India and Bangladesh.

Feeling so many emotions, I couldn't bear the thought of Wally being left in this horrible situation. I looked at John and Agnes Gabriel who I loved like second parents and implored for them to be released. I had a swelling in my throat and started to cry knowing I might never see the Gabriels or my husband again. I didn't know if I was being taken off to be shot or be set free. I felt conflicted with guilt since I was being released. Part of me wanted to stay to help them. I still couldn't conceive that I would be set free without them. I thought they were taking me off the plane to shoot me as I walked down the stairs to my death.

But when I saw the approaching Red Cross Van a rush of expectancy filled me! My heart almost leaped out of my chest. I'm being set free! I took in a large breath and said out loud, "I'm going to live, I'm going to live!" Exhilaration hit me and I let out a holler. I didn't care how hot it was. I ran to the van as fast I could.

The knowledge that I was going to live gave me such a rush of adrenaline that it overwhelmed me with happiness. I was free! I was going to see my little boys again! I was still alive! A deep emotion of thankfulness washed over me. I thanked God for his protection and will always remember the overwhelming feeling of relief and gratefulness to be alive.

The five of us were driven to the airport terminal. It was crazy! Several reporters from Reuters and the AP press corps surrounded me holding their microphones in my face and asking questions like, "Is it true you are a Hollywood Actress? How old are you?"

"Oh Goodness, I thought, I almost lost my life and you are asking me such inane questions? What kind of people are you?"

Several men in different uniforms, airline officials and government representatives, shouted questions all at once. The press asked me if there was anything that gave me a clue as to how they carried their guns onboard. I was about to say I was aware of the yellow boxes carried by the stewardess on board. Perhaps that is how they were brought in, but I noticed a man in the blue JAL uniform shake his head back and forth like he was saying, "NO! Don't say anything about it." I took his cue and dropped the subject.

The press bombarded me with more questions when a tall, American man introduced himself as the Attaché for the Agriculture Minister and said to please follow him to meet the American Ambassador, Ed Masters. They took me to a private room away from everyone else where several American CIA agents waited. They showed me three or four large spiral notebooks filled with photographs of known terrorists. They asked me to identify any of them. Since the terrorist had on the red and white scarves, I never saw their faces. I only saw the leader who I recognized immediately when they showed me his photo. They knew Marouka, and I confirmed he was the leader of this terrorist hijacking.

They informed me that Captain hijacker, Maruoka had trained most of the Japanese Red Army, a leftist terrorist group that emerged in the late 1960's. Since 1972 the Red Army has mounted several other attacks, including hijacking a Japan Air Lines plane from Amsterdam to Tokyo in 1973 attacking the Japanese Embassy in Kuala Lumpur, Malaysia, in 1975, and now this flight from Bombay to Dhaka, Bangladesh, in 1977.

The Red Army is described as insane by other terrorist groups since the massacre of 1972. They had no regard for human life. They killed 14 of their members and used self-criticism sessions using lynching, beating and knife attacks. Some members were left to die on stakes and froze to death. The Red Army called hyper Koshi or death by defeatist; the idea was if a comrade has enough purity, they will survive the beatings.

They asked me to identify the guns the terrorist carried, how many held hand grenades, and to describe the explosives on the floor. I told them they all held hand grenades. They needed to get a real picture to decide if storming the airplane was an option.

After debriefing me, they drove me down Madani Avenue to our American Embassy. All the buildings looked old, no modern sky scrapers. The streets were clean, with not one piece of trash anywhere. I was told the Bangladesh people were so poor they would pick up anything, even a can and make something out of it. I observed only men on the streets, but the few women I saw in the airport were dressed in colorful long dresses.

Our Embassy's red brick rectangle building looked like a fortress. I was so happy to be an American and be safe on our home turf. Our Ambassador, Ed Masters, met me and asked numerous questions about the hijackers. I told them there were five that I knew but felt there were two women in their group even though they never revealed themselves. One of the Ambassador's assistants brought me some food and an orange drink, Fanta. It tasted awful but at that point, I was glad to be drinking anything.

Ambassador Ed Masters told me, "We tried to give food to the plane after you were released but the hijackers refused, thinking it might have dope in it to put them to sleep."

He continued, "The leader of the terrorist group is Mr. Maruoka. He is well known. That is why he didn't cover his face. He was the second in command on the JAL747 that was hijacked before. He was supposed to go to Haifa but the head hijacker was killed in a hand grenade explosion on that plane. It was this 747 he flew to Benghazi and out of frustration, blew up the plane. A woman, Fusako Shignobu who they called, The Queen, was the leader of the Japanese Red Army and was giving orders from Lebanon.

I felt a new panic for the passengers learning how dangerous Marouka was.

"The terrorists are demanding the release of twelve of their comrades who were in Japanese jails. Three comrades have refused to leave. They had served most of their jail terms and didn't want to rejoin the Red Army."

The Ambassador looked tired. He had been awake all night also. He sighed, "If all goes well, Japan might agree to find all the comrades that they asked to be released. But they are in jails all over Japan. Air Vice Marshall Mahmud told the hijackers that it would take more time to find them all and arrange their transport to Dacca. This will take time, many hours, many days.

"Marouka demanded to have tape recordings of their comrade's voices who refused to come back to them. He didn't believe the negotiator and accused him of just stalling."

Officials debriefed me for a couple of hours, picking out pictures that might help identify the weapons. During the time I was kept hostage I was stalwart but now I felt I was falling apart. The experience took a toll on me, reality that my husband was still on the plane set in and I had gone into shock. I shuddered and my teeth chattered. The doctor said the long period without food and water caused dehydration. They summoned a doctor who recommended that I get some sleep.

Once the Embassy staff brought me a sandwich and lemon-laced water; they lead me to a bedroom.

I tried to sleep but anxiety overpowered me. I wanted to know about my husband and the other hostages. I felt uncomfortable knowing I was safe and that the others may die. They fed me soup, took my vitals, then released me to go to the hotel. I refused a sedative because of my baby. I needed to know what was happening with the others. Survivor guilt set in. A member of the Embassy drove me to the hotel.

The InterContinental Hotel was close to the airport. Large fans spun on the ceiling, furnishings were modest, staff was polite. My suite was plain. There was no frills, no luxurious touches, but clean. A table served as a desk and for meals and I had a perfect view of the airport from my window. A radio station was adjacent to the hotel.

Two CIA men instructed me how to use a two-way radio so I could listen to the dialogue between the plane and the tower. I strained to hear through the static.

The assistant to the Ambassador instructed me not to leave my room unless accompanied by my bodyguard who stood outside my room with a rifle. I smiled awkwardly at the young Bangladeshi and locked the door.

*CHAPTER SEVEN*

# DIAMONDS

**S**oon there was a knock on my door. A man from Japanese Airlines wished to speak to me. He entered. He was the man who shook his head at me at the airport when I mentioned the stewardesses had carried yellow boxes on board.

I offered him tea.

"Thank you for not mentioning the yellow boxes. They were full of diamonds."

I nearly dropped the tea pot. "What do you mean?" I queried.

"Our airline has a contract with the gem cutters, and we send diamonds three times a day to Bangkok. One plane didn't fly so we doubled the amount on your flight. Only one shipment was insured. Over six million dollars' worth of diamonds are on the plane!"

I was stunned. I had seen two men discussing the yellow boxes in Bombay.

"We did not want the terrorists to know the diamonds were on the plane."

"I saw the attendants put the yellow boxes in the compartments above the terrorist's seats!" Oh my, I'm happy you warned me the way you did!"

"We cannot reveal the diamonds are on the plane. Newspapers would run with the story. Please do not tell anyone about the diamonds."

I assured I wouldn't tell anyone, he finished his tea and left.

It became unbearable not knowing about the hostages. I worried about my husband and our friends. I hoped no hostages were hurt. They had no food or water for two days. The agony of waiting knowing how uncomfortable the passengers were contributed more anxiety. I listened closely to the radio for any tidbit of information trying to feel connected to the captives.

I heard Marouka ask the tower to send them fruit cups, juice, empty food containers and newspapers.

"Now about the newspaper I am thinking whether I will be able to get the permission to give you the newspaper or not because newspapers always tell lies most of the time they are not correct."

JRA: "We like to get the information from you. We asked for the newspapers because we like to know the impact of our action."

Tower: "I will collect 23 newspapers and read out the news items to you."

JRA: "I agree, and if you can please send us alcohol you understand?"

Tower: "What do you want?"

JRA: "Alcohol. Alcohol."

Tower: "Alcohol? Whiskey?"

JRA: "Alcohol!"

Tower: "Danke, you want a whiskey or others?"

JRA: "Not whiskey, for medical use. You understand?"

Tower: "Oh you want spirits!! You want Methylene spirit for medical use.

JRA: "Yeah, yeah!"

Some in the tower said: "They are afraid they will get cholera!"

Later I heard the JRA ask, "Why my three comrades in jail do not want to come here? We want evidence that they refused. We have suspected that Japan did not inform the three.

We want evidence that this is true with their own intentions! Bring us tape recordings so I can hear their voices and you are not lying to us!"

This took more time.

It helped to know that something was being done to satisfy these radical terrorists but no one on the plane had any hope of being rescued. I called and asked our Ambassador, Ed Masters if he could influence the negotiating team to ask the hijackers to inform the passengers that the Japanese Government was considering their demands. I wanted the passengers to know if they met the terrorist's demands there was hope of being released. That might delay the hijackers from killing any of the passengers.

The radio went silent. I stepped into the cool shower, water ran down my back and legs. How good it felt to get the perspiration out of my hair and have solitude for a few moments. I crawled into the bed and prayed for the passenger's safety then slept for a few hours.

# CHAPTER EIGHT

# RELEASED PASSENGERS

**I** woke up hearing on the radio that the embassy set up for me the hijackers speaking to the tower.

JRA: "You have taken too long to give me a simple answer."

Tower: "We have a lot of work to do together I will request you, please answer the question! Simply yes or no so that I can quickly do all things required to help you solve the problem, so that you can take off to your destination."

JRA: "Please, these long talks are going to delay."

Tower: "It is a matter of principle that the passengers be released now, but how many do you need for your safety is a matter of your decision. You have some idea as to what is my profession. I will tell you my name later on, please help me."

Air Vice Marshall A.G. Mahmud continued. "I have only one piece of information. The Japanese Government has requested for a special flight from Tokyo to Dhaka. I'm trying to do things so that the time is short as possible. Please remember we are doing everything to make things happen as early as possible."

As the negotiations dragged on, the terrorists released five more passengers and then the next day eleven more hostages.

For four days the jet sat on the smoldering runway while Japan and Bangladesh negotiated the exchange of hostages for the ransom money and the Japanese prisoners. Although the hijackers refused to release all the hostages at once, the exchange seemed to be proceeding well.

I turned on the radio and heard, "It was reported John Gabriel was singled out by the hijackers because he was Jewish. His associates at his bank said that Gabriel is a Christian Armenian along with his wife, Agnes. Among the other Americans still held hostage is Walter Karabian, a prominent California Democratic leader. He was on his honeymoon with his famous bride, actress Carole Wells, who starred in many television series and movies including "Funny Lady" was one of the five hostages freed."

To avoid going crazy, I tried writing about this experience. Trying to calm my mind, I wrote copious notes of the conversations from the plane to the tower and visa versa. A knock on the door interrupted my writing. A sexy, big-busted, red headed, American woman arrived at my hotel suite.

She said with a big Dallas smile, "Hi Honey, I'm Mary. Our Ambassador asked me to bring you some clothes. I brought you a long dress, pants and a white blouse." Not waiting for me to invite her in, she strolled in as if she owned the place. Mary was quite stunning, tall, and full-bodied with long red hair. She handed me a hairbrush and lipstick.

"Thank you for bringing me your clothes. I'm grateful to receive these."

"Honey, Asian women are small with tiny breasts. I'm the only woman in Dacca who has a voluptuous figure like yours!"

She put both her hands on her breast and held them bouncing them up and down. "Yes, I guess the Ambassador remembered me!"

Mary laughed, sauntered over to the phone, and ordered a bottle of champagne. She was friendly and talked incessantly. After a few hours, she told me she was having a roaring affair with one of our CIA guys who was assigned to take care of me. When he arrived to check in on me, he flirted with her outrageously.

"My husband is gone. He won't be back until the hijack situation is over. He's a pilot and gone all the time." She explained trying to excuse her actions while stretching her arms and legs as if she were practicing in a dance studio.

Later that afternoon, my CIA guardian came back. He asked if I needed anything. "Yes, how about something to brush my teeth and wash my hair, anything!"

He didn't pay attention to me. His attention was completely on Mary and couldn't keep his hands off her. I tried to listen to the conversation on the radio. Seeing I was distracted, he started kissing Mary and slipped his hand up the back of her dress caressing her buttocks. She pressed her ample bosoms against him beckoning him to continue touching her. The two of them started kissing, acting as if I weren't even there! Mary rubbed her hand on his privates, and he was in full bloom. He was hot and ready to have sex with her in my hotel room! The agent picked her up and moved into my bedroom. He didn't even ask. He just shut the door leaving me alone. I was so embarrassed I didn't know what to do! Thank God, I had a living room suite.

Not liking this situation, I left my hotel suite to look for a toothbrush and toiletries, since our bags were on the plane. My guard walked beside me with his rifle. The streets were full of bicycles and carts. Young men peddled their colorful painted rickshaws, with cut-outs appliqué on the hoods with brass vases replete with paper or plastic flowers.

"This is our standard transportation, very few automobiles on the roads." My Bangladesh bodyguard told me, "the boys peddling have short lives. They die by the time they are thirty years old from starvation!"

Feeling sorry for the skinny drivers I pondered what he told me. We walked up the street in silence. I felt safe with my bodyguard who carried a rifle and wore a bandolier belt full of bullets across his chest. The bandolier belts reminded me of Mexico's Past President, Miguel Aleman Valdes' soldiers who wore them when I was in Mexico.

I had the pleasure of being the president's guest at his home in Acapulco where his guards wore bandolier belts even while we waterskied. The memory of our delightful times in Mexico with the Corqueras and the Alemans gave me a brief moment of happiness.

We walked through the old buildings and narrow streets for several blocks searching for a toothbrush and some toiletries, but there was nothing remotely like a drug store. Feeling odd I realized I was the only woman on the streets. The men stared at me in wonderment as if I were a Christmas tree! My blond hair and red nail polish fascinated them. They were enthralled and kept staring at me, not disrespectfully but with curiosity. Thank goodness I wore my jeans and tennis shoes. If I wore a dress and exposed my arms or legs, they would have stoned me!

I ached all over from being so traumatized. The air's humidity felt sticky in my lungs. It was hard to breathe. I stalled giving the two lovers in my hotel suite more time. I felt disconnected from the plane and didn't like being away from the radio in my room. The debilitating heat drove me back to the hotel. I was upset that the CIA agent and Mary were using my bedroom for their affair. I didn't need any more problems.

When we returned to the hotel, my guard told me, "I am going back to the airport to see if there is anything I can do or find out. Please don't leave again. I'll be back later."

I walked up to my room and told the couple, "You're taking advantage of my horrible situation. Don't use my room again. Here, I am worried sick that the terrorists might kill my husband and friends and you two are carrying on as if nothing dangerous is happening!"

The CIA agent felt ashamed that he was thoughtless and apologized. He offered to find me a toothebrush and toothpaste. It was a great act of kindness saying "I'm sorry" since I hadn't brushed my teeth since I left Egypt.

They both left me alone to listen to the conversation between the plane and tower. I could hear the impatient hijackers demanding the negotiators move faster.

Ed Masters told me, Don't tell anyone or talk to the newsmen." He confided, "One delay occurred because the Japanese government only had two million dollars cash in their banks. A plane from New York is flying four million in one hundred-dollar bills to Japan adding more time, but no one can know that."

As more passengers were released, I started filling up one of the Ambassador's cars taking food and drinks from the hotel to the hospital. How primitive it was! The rooms were pathetic: no running water, just a bare bed, a paper carton for a wastebasket and no bathroom.

Most of the Arab passengers now recovering in the hospital didn't speak English, but they gestured from their beds handing me gold rings, money, and more of their precious belongings for me to keep. They were afraid someone would steal them in the hospital while they slept. I felt so badly for the dehydrated passengers who needed medical attention. I encouraged them to drink the Fanta and helped them get medical treatment. The Bangladesh people tried to assist me. I was thankful for the extra hands. I couldn't understand the passenger's language, but their eyes showed me their gratitude.

I took everything they gave me and placed it with the other treasures in the hotel safe. The lobby was relatively quiet, so I returned to my suite and ordered dinner. All I could eat the entire time was their Mulligatawny soup, an English soup with origins in Indian cuisine. After my light meal, I called the embassy but there were no new updates on my husband, Wally or the other passengers. I felt lonely and missed my husband. I took a shower and crawled into bed.

## Photo Collection: Carole's life in photos before the event

*Wedding L.A. MAY 1977*

*Wally & Carole—Armenia, 1977*

*Carole, Hubert Humphrey and John Gabriel*

*John and Agnes Gabriel, with the Pope in Armenia 1977*

*John & Agnes Gabriel with us on airplane before hijacking,*
*image of JAL Airlines*

## Career Photos

*Carole singing and dancing on stage at 3,*
*as core cast of TV series, National Velvet*

*DEB STAR Ball with Bob Hope & Joan Crawford, Carole and*
*Larry Doheny arriving Beverly Hills Hotel wedding reception 1963*

*French Magazine Cover photo 1962*

*Carole & Gary Vinson TV Series Pistols 'n Petticoats,*
*playing Norma Butler in Funny Lady*

71

*With President Nixon at the White House*

*Playing Norma in Funny Lady*

*Carole with Barbra Streisand, Roddy McDowall,*
*in Funny Lady with James Cann & Matt Emery*

*Ingrid Bergman, Nat Cohen & Carole—*
*Academy Awards winning 13 for Murder on the Orient Express*

*Edward Laurence Doheny V aka Sean
and Ryan Robert Doheny*

*Sean 8 and Ryan 6 with Wally, Carole
and John Gabriel at our wedding May1977*

## Newspaper Articles

*Californians Article – September 29, 1977*

*Japanese Terrorists Threaten Killings*

## HIJACKERS' DEMANDS

Continued from First Page

mother, Mrs. Charles Krueger, said. Mrs. Krueger, of Granada Hills, said her son's wife, Marian, remained at the ashram where she teaches children, and was to rejoin her husband in six months. Krueger, who attended Alemany High School in Granada Hills and graduated from the University of Colorado, formerly taught at Bernardo Junior High School in Los Angeles, his mother said.

State Department sources were reported to have disclosed that Gabriel was singled out by the terrorists for execution because "he looked Jewish." Actually, Gabriel is a Christian of Armenian ancestry, according to Walter Hemphill, vice president of the Garfield Bank. Hemphill said that Gabriel had been president of the bank since it started in 1955.

The hijackers, in a statement given to airport officials here, said they were determined to "free the Japanese people from oppression." The statement listed what it called atrocities by the Japanese government, which was described as having imperialist power over people, making them worse than machines.

The terrorists issued their execution threat even after the Tokyo government agreed to meet the demand for $6 million ransom, but said it would need time to consider the demand to release the hijackers' comrades from prison.

Tokyo's decision to free the nine prisoners was announced by Chief Cabinet Secretary Sunao Sonoda, who said the decision had been conveyed to the hijackers aboard

the airliner parked on the runway here.

Sonoda said the hijackers had demanded that the nine radicals be flown to Dacca within 18 hours of the decision to release them, but that the government had told them it would be impossible to meet this deadline.

The hijackers, informed of Tokyo's decision, insisted they wanted their released comrades in Dacca today. They said they then would free Japanese, Pakistanis, women and children among the hostages, and after that, take off for an unnamed destination, releasing the remaining hostages at airports along the way.

Sonoda told reporters the Japanese government had decided to bow to the hijackers' demands "for humanitarian reasons and for safety of the passengers and crew."

Bangladesh army troops surrounded the hijacked plane, but stayed at a distance of 200 yards from the jetliner in accordance with the hijackers' demands.

An airport official said there may be more than the two hijackers originally reported.

The hijackers referred to the seizure as a "military operation" and told negotiators that of the 155 passengers and crew hostages "some are friends, some not."

Among the passengers were 84 Japanese and 57 foreigners, mostly of Indian, Chinese and Indonesian nationality.

The Red Army is the most notorious of Japan's ultraleftist terrorist bands, but most of its operations have been outside the country, and police have linked it with radical Palestinian groups in Lebanon.

*Hijackers' Demands*

---

Dacca, Thursday, September 29, 1977

# The Bangladesh Times

**They're two top JRA leaders**

## Japanese govt concedes $ 6 million ransom demand only

### JAL DC-8 hijackers set 5 am for the first execution

# High drama at Dacca airport

**By Times Staffers**

Two of the nine prisoners whose release the hijackers of Japanese DC-8 airliner sought were Fusako Shigenobu and Haruo Wako, two of the most important leaders of Japanese Red Army faction...

**Council of Advisers meets**

**All passengers underwent security checks at Paris, Athens**

Japanese Airlines DC-8 type aircraft landed at Dacca Airport Crashed Tower at 5 a.m. this morning on expiry of the second extended deadline that they plan to execute John Cabriel...

Who are the JRA ?

Indonesian Minister among hostages

Egypt asks USSR for moratorium on debt

Abbas leaves for Delhi to resume talks

*High Drama At DACCA Airport*

# Japan Hijackers Extend Ransom Deadline---Today

DACCA, Bangladesh (AP) — Masked terrorists holding 146 hostages aboard a hijacked Japanese jetliner at Dacca airport agreed Friday to give the Japanese government one more day to meet their demands.

Air Vice Marshal Mahmoud, who had been conducting negotiations, said the five hijackers extended their Thursday midnight deadline to 4 a.m. Saturday (3 p.m. PDT Friday) as the siege entered its third day.

Mahmoud said he explained to the gunmen that the Japanese government was having difficulty arranging for the $6 million ransom and the release from Japanese prisons of nine persons, most of them terrorists.

The hijackers, identified as members of the ultra-leftist Japanese Red Army and said to be armed with guns and grenades, released five passengers Thursday, including Mrs. Carole Wells Karabian, wife of former Fresno and State Assemblyman Walter Karabian.

The gunmen were still holding 14 crew members and 132 passengers, including 10 Americans.

They have threatened to begin killing their hostages one by one, starting with California banker John Gabriel, unless the ransom money and the prisoners are delivered.

A spokesman for the Japanese cabinet said the government was trying to round up the ransom money in New York after the hijackers' demands for 60,000 U.S. $100 bills. The government also was canvassing the nine prisoners, the spokesman said, but two reportedly refused to accept the offer of freedom.

Heavy security was imposed at the Dacca international airport, isolating the hijacked DC-8, and foreign correspondents and photographers were barred.

Mrs. Karabian, a former Hollywood actress,

**See Hijackers, Back Page**

Mrs. Carole Karabian
UPI Telept

*Carole Hijackers Deadline*

*Hijackers Free 5 Hostages*

*Hijackers Free Wife of Former Assemblyman*

77

*Weeping Heiress Tells Story*

*Death Was Minutes Away*

## Mrs. Karabian, Hostage on Jet, Has Miscarriage

Actress Carole Wells Karabian, one of 156 hostages aboard a Japan Air Lines plane hijacked two weeks ago, was released Wednesday from St. John's Hospital in Santa Monica after treatment for a miscarriage.

Her husband, former Assemblyman Walter Karabian, said Wednesday there was "no doubt in my mind" the ordeal aboard the aircraft at the hands of Japanese Red Army terrorists caused his pregnant wife to lose their baby.

"But I am reluctant to talk about something that is a very personal family matter and my wife has been through a very anguishing experience," he said. "Bangladesh, the hijacking, all of that. It was the worst thing we've ever been through in our lives."

The Karabians and friends, Montebello banker John Gabriel and his wife, Agnes, were traveling together aboard the JAL plane when it was hijacked after taking off from Bombay for Bangkok Sept. 28.

Mrs. Karabian, 35, and four other Americans were released the following day but the Gabriels and Karabian were among the last hostages to be freed.

"I was so scared that I never saw such terror in all my life," Mrs. Karabian said at the time of her release in Dacca, Bangladesh. "They kept screaming and yelling at us and warning us that they would shoot us if we did anything wrong."

The hijackers surrendered Oct. 3 to Algerian authorities after flying from Dacca, where a settlement was negotiated.

As Carole Wells, Mrs. Karabian appeared in NBC's National Velvet television series in 1962 and in the movies "Funny Girl" and "Thunder of the Drums."

## Ex-Teacher Gets 60 Days for Intercourse With Coed, 15

Former junior high-school teacher Hector Aguilar was sentenced Wednesday to 60 days in county jail for having sexual intercourse with a 15-year-old female student.

Norwalk Superior Judge John L. Donnelian also placed the 35-year-old Aguilar on three years' probation and recommended that the prisoner be put on work furlough while in jail.

*Mrs. Karabian, hostage on jet, has miscarriage*

## Banker Terrorized For Hijackers' Error

Fresno Bee a d., Oct. 5, 1977

TOKYO (AP) — An ailing American banker aboard a hijacked Japanese airliner collapsed at gunpoint and was left unconscious for hours because the terrorists thought he was a Jewish friend of President Carter, a fellow hijack victim said Tuesday.

Walter Karabian, former Democratic leader of the California Legislature, said the hijackers mistook banker John Gabriel for a friend of Carter "because I persuaded them to let me send a telex to the President, the U.S. ambassador in Bangladesh and five congressmen on his behalf.

"That made him their first target," he added in an interview with The Associated Press. Gabriel, not a Jew but an Armenian Christian, was named by the hijackers as the first hostage to be shot if their demands were not met.

Meanwhile in Algiers a Japanese Air Lines DC8 picked up the last 12 hostage passengers and seven crew members Tuesday to fly them to Tokyo, the original destination of their trip.

The hijackers, who seized the JAL plane over India last Wednesday, surrendered Monday to Algerian authorities after a flight from Dacca, Bangladesh, where the hijack settlement was negotiated. Algerian officials declined to say what has happened to the hijackers, their six comrades released from Japanese prisons or to the $6 million ransom paid by the Japanese government.

Karabian, who was among hostages released Sunday, said that as Thursday, the day after the plane was seized, the hijackers took his 65-year-old Gabriel to the cockpit and closed the door.

In an earlier interview Gabriel had said of his treatment: "I had the worst end of it. They were determined to kill me....There were three terrorists in the cockpit, three guns at my head. They fired two shots into the air through the window."

Karabian said, "I heard from John later the terrorists threatened him saying 'You capitalist, you shall be the first one to be executed,' or something. After getting out of the cockpit, he collapsed and lay on the floor for two to three hours.

"We could do nothing, because the hijackers never permitted us to stand up or take care of him. But Dr. Masayuki Bukan, a Japanese doctor aboard, gave him medical care and then recommended that the hijackers release him, which they later did."

Gabriel and Karabian, with their wives, were on a round-the-world trip when the hijackers took command of the DC8 10 minutes after it took off from Bombay for Bangkok last Wednesday, he said. Gabriel, who calls Karabian "my adopted son," is a leader of California's Armenian community.

Mrs. Karabian, former actress Carol Wells Karabian, was released Thursday and Gabriel, on Friday. Karabian said he believes the Japanese government took "the cleverest, most inexpensive and humanitarian way" to solve the problem by paying $6 million in ransom and releasing six persons from Japanese jails as demanded by the hijackers.

"Otherwise the world would have said, after the plane was blown up, 'What kind of people are the Japanese to permit such a human loss to simply trying to save $6 million?' The aircraft alone is more expensive than that."

Japanese Deputy Minister of Transport Rajime Ishii said in Algiers he doubted that Tokyo would ask for the return of the hijackers or the ransom money.

Ishii, who expressed his government's appreciation for Algeria's help in resolving the hijack, to which there were originally 201 hostages, said that while not speaking for the government he "will personally that we have asked the Algerian government for so much in this affair, we may not be in a position" to ask more.

*Mrs. Karabian lands in Tokyo.*
*UPI Telephoto*

*Banker Terrorized For Hijackers Error*

## Californian marked for execution

LOS ANGELES (UPI) — Some acquaintances suspect bank president John Gabriel, marked for execution by leftist Japanese skyjackers in Bangladesh, may have joked his way into trouble by kidding that he was a good friend of President Carter — which isn't true.

Gabriel, president of the Garfield Bank, was among 155 hostages aboard a Japan Air Lines jetliner hijacked yesterday.

Thirteen of the 156 hostages were Americans, including two of the four released by the hijackers. One of those released was actress Carole Wells, a traveling companion of Gabriel's and wife of former California Assemblyman Walter Karabian, a Los Angeles lawyer

—See Back Page, Col. 1

AP and UPI Photos

**Californian banker John Gabriel was marked as the first hostage to be executed by skyjackers at Dacca (above)**

*Californian Marked for Execution*

## Released Hostage Calls Flight 'Absolute Terror'

LOS ANGELES, Oct. 2 (AP) — Terrorists who hijacked a Japan Air Lines jet over India last week boarded the airplane at the Bombay airport "carrying pistols and hand grenades," according to a passenger who was among hostages released from the plane today.

There are no metal detectors at the Bombay airport, and as long as "airports and nations permit that kind of conduct," said Walter Karabian, a former California state assemblyman who was among the hostages held by members of the ultraleftist Japanese Red Army for nearly five days.

In a telephone interview with station KNX from Dacca, Bangladesh, Karabian said that what began as a "very pleasant flight" from Paris to Tokyo became an experience of "absolute terror" for the passengers and crew of the hijacked jetliner.

He said the terrorists "left no doubt that they would shoot to kill." Karabian, 39, and his wife, former actress Carole Wells, planned to return to Los Angeles Tuesday along with Montebello, Calif., banker John Gabriel and his wife, Agnes. The two couples were in Bangkok late tonight after being released from the hijacked DC-8.

More than 100 of the hostages were eventually freed after Japan paid a $6 million ransom and released six of the terrorists' comrades from Japanese prisons. At least 30 hostages were still in the plane when it took off from Dacca for the Middle East today.

Of the remaining hostages, three are Americans, officials said.

Three other Americans still believed to be aboard the plane are Eric Weiss of San Francisco, Thomas F. Phalen, a San Francisco resident on assignment with the U.S. State Department, and W.D. McLean, a San Francisco corporation executive.

Mrs. Karabian, 35, was among the hostages, released Thursday. The Gabriels were freed yesterday.

## Hijackers Fly To Damascus, Free 17 Hostages

A hijacked Japanese airliner flew from Bangladesh to Kuwait and then to Syria, Monday, and 17 more hostages were released at the two Middle Eastern stops.

Only 12 of the 166 passengers on the Japan Air Lines DC-8 when it was hijacked remained aboard, the Airline announced in Tokyo. There were also seven Japanese crew members aboard, along with the five original hijackers and six of their Red Army comrades who were freed from prison in exchange for the release of 60 hostages on Sunday.

Seven hostages, reported to be ill, were freed in Kuwait. Japanese and Syrian sources said 10 others were freed in Syria, and two of the three remaining hostages were among them. The identity of the Americans was not immediately known, however.

Both Kuwait and Syria initially refused to let the plane land, relenting only for humanitarian reasons. The plane was refueled in Kuwait and the hijackers asked for fuel and supplies in Syria.

A Japanese Foreign Ministry spokesman in Tokyo said it was assumed that the hijackers would continue their journey in quest of a country that would give them asylum.

The Japan Broadcasting Corporation (NHK) quoted one of the hostages released at Kuwait as saying the hijackers had discussed a flight to Damascus, and then Tripoli, Libya, and Algeria.

The plane took off Sunday night.

See HIJACK, A13, Col. 2

*Released hostage calls flight 'absolute terror'*
*& hijackers fly to Damascus, free 17 hostages*

*Carole – Appearance in Japanese Newspaper*

*Hijackers Surrender Headline*

A-2    THE SAN DIEGO UNION    Th

## AT A GLANCE

# Hijackers Failed To Notice Gems

Compiled from The San Diego Union's News Services

LOS ANGELES — Nearly $2 million worth of diamonds went unnoticed by hijackers who held a Japan Air Lines plane and up to 156 hostages for five days, a returning hostage said yesterday.

"I think to this moment the hijackers are not aware that they had $2 million worth of diamonds sitting there right across from their command center," said former California Assemblyman Walter J. Karabian, 39, who held an airport news conference after returning home. "These diamonds were in packages put right on top of the seat where the stewardess generally sits in that area right across from the galley and remained there in these plain unmarked packages during the entire hijacking episode.

"And when we were released on the fifth day, one of the stewardesses just casually picked up these boxes and walked off the airplane with them." The diamonds, he said, were later valued at $1,850,000, Karabian said.

*Failed to Notice Gems*

*JAL Airlines*

*Hijackers Portraits*

CHAPTER NINE

# COOPERATION

The static of the Tower radio awakened me. Here is my best recollection of the dialogue between the JRA and the Air Control Tower in Dhaka.

Tower: "Danke this is Dhaka, good morning to you."

JRA: "Good morning."

Tower: "I hope it's a good morning."

JRA: "We will release all Indian and Pakistani passengers when our demand is met! The number of Pakistani people is six, Indian two, and we will release all Japanese women, number is 35 and Singapore woman one, Korean woman one, New Zealand woman one, American woman one, Brazilian woman one, Egyptian woman one."

Mahmud in the Tower: "Danke if you don't mind I want to ask you a question, your objective should be completed to a great extent. I do not know to what extent you were going to be satisfied, but it will be to a great extent satisfied."

JRA: "We demand release of twelve of our JRA prisoners. Second, we demand $6 million. Unless you accept the first amount we start executing Americans and then the other hostages. This is our final announcement." Their radio went silent.

Ambassador Ed Masters called to tell me, "Japan's Prime Minister as the central figure called together his cabinet. Everybody has been discussing their terms although to accept this demand is unbearable. On the other hand, lives of 142 passengers and 14-flight crew, when Japan considers that safety of the country, is not the only thing to consider. At 8p.m. we told the criminals regarding the first amount we accept to discuss it."

§

Hours later:

Tower: "Danke this is your friend."

JRA: "Go ahead."

Tower: "If you look out your window, you will see a special Japanese aircraft has landed. It is on the runway now."

JRA: "Yes I have seen it."

Tower: "We must go, through the whole procedure very realistically and carefully. Therefore, you should remain at the radio and maintain continuous listening and watch."

I listened to Air Vice Marshal Mahmud on the two-way radio patiently repeating everything the JRA said. Very slowly he discussed how to appeal to the terrorist sentiment, and Mahmud was trying to treat them with respect to keep the hostages safe.

Mahmud: "I would like to express my opinion on your views about using the passengers until you get home. You do not wish to release as a guarantee. My personal feeling is that it is not necessary to do this. The moment you leave Bangladesh probably you'll never hear my voice, but I think still there can be a possibility we can definitely try and try and try again to find a positive way of meeting your requirements. I'll take one more minute to speak again, thank you."

I heard Mahmud speak. "If you look out your window you will see special Japanese aircraft has landed. It is on the runway now. Please confirm everything I asked for is complete. The steps have not gone down yet. It will only go after I clear. Until I clear, nobody will come out except the foreign secretary, and after the foreign secretary has come out, the air steps will be moved."

JRA "Ok."

Mahmud: "Steps will not remain close to the aircraft. It will remain about 20 feet away. It will not open until I say.

Any aircraft coming will be diverted. Do we allow foreign secretary?"

JRA: "Yes."

Mahmud switched off the microphone to the plane. I heard him say to his team, "He won't go out now. WAIT! WHERE IS THAT HELICOPTER GOING? COME ON! Sir! Rasheed, find out what they're doing. You told him to switch off? How did you tell them? Radio who?"

I could only hear Mahmud's upset voice. "Squad leader if they don't switch off you send somebody and get everybody off. NOBODY NEAR HELICOPTER! NOBODY should be there! SEE TO IT PLEASE! Other people I don't know are not going to be allowed. Not anybody to move! Please go downstairs. SEAL IT OFF. WHO DO THEY THINK THEY ARE?"

Again silence.

JRA: "We now want to add a few passengers more if you allow to free them, over."

Tower: "Roger... give me one more minute to just have a glass of water. OK, you also have a glass of water then we shall talk again."

JRA: "Roger."

Again, I heard the tower turn off communications with the plane.

Tower: Speaking to the others in the tower, "OK, now he is showing a willingness because he understands he's not going to get away just by releasing 52 passengers.... Wait! Who gave instructions? WHO IS THAT? GET IN TOUCH! Who was that Burma Eastern Oil asking about refueling? TELL BURMA EASTERN NO REFUELING, NO REFUELING: NOT EVEN ANY WATER. NOTHING WILL GO."

Turning back on the radio to the plane, Tower: "Danke, I am happy to note that you want to discuss the release of more passengers."

JRA: "Yes." In his broken English, "But additional number is only three hostages, over."

Tower: "That number that you have decided three is not acceptable to me. It is not acceptable to me. Please understand this. Are you ready to discuss?"

JRA: "Negative, we release three more passengers. Our patience is finished now. We will not bargain with the Japanese regime. Will never bargain with Japanese. We have your cooperation and support, but this is different matter. We are very tired. You said it'd be just half-hour, but more than five hours now. We are losing confidence in you. We had much confidence in you 'till today."

Another voice spoke from the tower: "Hello Danke, this afternoon we arrived. I'm the Japanese government representative. Upon reading your demands, we brought the people you requested. We also brought the ransom, but about the transfer and where to transfer going forward regarding this matter, please reconsider because this has become a crucial international issue. We are listening to your demands. We are trying to meet them sincerely at least start trusting us."

JRA: "Shut up! We begin execution. We don't wait anymore! We lose enough time! We are commandos; we already waited almost 6 hours. It's enough, don't speak! We are soldiers. We don't let you make that stupid action! Over."

Tower conversation, "What did he say?"

Tower: "This is Dhaka tower. I have not understood your last sentence; please repeat. The plane is moving! PLANE IS MOVING!"

JRA: "I said we waited enough time now it's past six hours after landing of the special flight. What is the reason? We don't repeat our demand and waiting six hours for nothing! We are determined to begin our action."

Tower: "Fire station, quickly!"

JRA: "We don't like Japanese regime make stupid thing."

Tower: "Get down on the tarmac fast!"

JRA: "We don't wait anymore."

Tower conversation: "Hello? ALL TRANSPORT ON THE RUNWAY!"

JRA: "Meet our demand immediately. Our time limit has finished.

Tower conversation: "Hello? Who gave that order? Hello? Hold on hold on just because of transmission."

Tower: "Danke this is Dhaka tower."

Tower conversation: "Hold it. Hold everything."

JRA: "This is Danke."

Mahmud: "Just hold it. Plane moving to the right. Call him right now. CALL HIM! CRASH STAND TO TOWER! Crash stand to tower, crash stand to tower, hold on. Back it, BACK UP, BACK UP, back up!"

JRA: "What is happening?"

Tower: "We don't want them to go to airfield. Give threat if need be."

Tower: "Danke what is your intention now?"

JRA: "Now we are bringing a passenger over."

Tower: "Are you going to take off?"

JRA: "We begin execution, over."

Tower: "But you said that you would not do anything on our soil."

JRA: "Our demand is still blood. It should be ready six hours ago, nothing."

Tower: "Danke we will close this taxi track. You'll not be able to taxi. You stand there on the runway."

Tower conversation: "Truck on the runway, close taxi track, close it immediately."

JRA: "Our plan to start shooting."

Tower: "YOU STAND THERE! STAND THERE NOW! Stop there now."

JRA: "Over."

Tower: "Danke stop there now."

JRA: "You agreed to send our demand."

Tower: "Don't turn into the taxi track!"

JRA: "You agreed to send our demands immediately right now, over."

Mahmud: "Crash standers, crash standers get in front. Everybody hold current position tell them to fill it further. Why the hell can't you just block? WHY DON'T YOU GET THE HELL OUT AND BLOODY WELL STOP THAT PLANE? Bloody fools blocked it from the north side as well, so plane cannot move. We need to talk to Okudaria."

Tower: "Danke are you going to come back to position?"

JRA: "Negative we heard Japanese regime behind you. Send here our Comrades and money right now."

Mahmud pleaded: "We are independent country. We could have stopped you from landing here. You said you are low on fuel and you crash if you did not land in here so we said OK. Now, you say Japanese government is behind us. This is wrong and you do not want to hurt our people. You do not want to create problems for our country."

JRA: "We do not hurt workers but we hurt bourgeois people it is duty of revolutionary soldiers!"

Mahmud pleaded: "Please come back to position I really request you, I beg you, please come back to position! This is not the thing to do for these poor people who had looked after you for 80 continuous hours and paid for everything. It is poor farmers' money. It is poor workers' money. It is poor man's money."

JRA: "I do appreciate. Show us some evidence."

Tower: "OK, OK. I'll show you evidence. I'll meet you. You just cannot betray me. For the last 80 hours I've talked to you without sleep. You come back to position. You can't betray me. You're a fighter. I tell you, I'm a fighter also."

After addressing his patience and tact, my admiration for Air Vice Marshall Mahmud soared. His patience, commanding discussions, and sensitivity—even with sleepless nights—made my heart appreciate how difficult his role played in this hostage drama.

# CHAPTER TEN

# DAY FOUR
# OUT OF CONTROL

**I** spent most of the time waiting in my hotel for word about my husband. It was miserable not knowing if my husband was hurt or hungry. I needed to know if he and the Gabriels were alright. Not knowing was agony.

To stay involved, I took detailed notes of the conversations between the Tower and the hijackers. Shots rang out. I rushed to the window. It sounded like fireworks coming from the radio station. I called the American ambassador. "Ed, there are gun shots outside my window!"

He assured me it was an uprising in another province several miles way.

"No, the shooting is right outside my window between two groups."

"What color uniforms are they wearing?"

I replied, "Some wearing blue uniforms, others brown. Oh wait, some blues are shooting other blues. Everyone is shooting each other!"

"Stay in your hotel, don't go outside, stay away from the hospital until I know what the situation is. Let me know if you see anything else. I'm sending you some of my staff to stay with you in case it gets worse."

I did as he told me and watched the fighting out my window when suddenly there was a loud knock on the door. My Bangladeshi guard rushed in my room frightened and wet with perspiration.

He blurted out, "There is chaos at the airport. A faction of the national air force took the opportunity to stage a coup to grab the $6 million ransom money. They killed everyone in the tower. I jumped from the window into the fern garden, which broke my fall." He continues, "The airport is on lockdown. They've blocked reporters and taken control. I fear for the hostages. The terrorists may panic and blow up the plane."

"Did they hurt Mahmud?" I inquired.

"No, he had just left to go downstairs, I don't know where he is or if he is safe. The airport had been put under siege when the men stormed up the circular staircase to the tower. There were dead bodies everywhere!"

I tried to understand the seriousness of the coup and what would happen to the hostages. If only I could speak to my husband. I gave my guard some water. He was terrified.

Then he said, "The hijackers shot out the window and held an American hostage as a shield. He was an old man."

I stiffened, thinking it was John Gabriel. "Oh my God!" I gasped, "Now what will happen to the people on the plane?" I feared for Wally's life.

"I have to go now. I'm sorry I must leave now." He said apologetically, "There might be bigger trouble."

I thanked him for coming to tell me the news and said I understood. I wondered if he would be safe on the streets, but I knew he had other important business. I tried to hear what the hijacker was yelling on the radio. I was terrified, sick, trembling. I threw up. Felt helpless and unable to do anything. My heart fell into pieces. I must not give up, I must think of something to help my husband!

Loud static from the Tower came across the two-way radio. I heard, "People with arms may approach your aircraft. My sincere request if they do approach aircraft you may call the tower. We will confirm who are authorized to be close to the plane. Save the lives of those ground crews who have been working with your aircraft for 5 days. We trust you without hesitation. Shoot those people to kill."

JRA: "I have understood that you have internal problems and some people are armed and many approaches. Your man is under the aircraft, and we confirm with you, if people are not from you, we shoot them. Is this correct?"

As I listened to the conversations between the tower and the JRA speaker, I understood the Bangladesh negotiator was telling the JRA terrorist to shoot one of the core air force members should they try to board the plane.

I could hear the hijackers screaming, "What's going on?" Who is shooting at us?" My knees buckled when I heard on the radio gun shots.

Vice Air Marshall Mahmud had disappeared and was no longer negotiating with the terrorist. There was silence from the tower. A sickening silence that left me disconnected from the plane.

I felt unsteady just staring at the radio trying to hear what was happening. My mind raced to different scenarios. Will they light the fuses on the explosives? Will they kill the hostages and themselves? I feared Wally would not be released, feared he may be killed. Our future plans disintegrated. I felt sick, unable to breathe. Again, I horrified that my husband would be killed.

I tried calling our ambassador. No one answered. My bodyguard was gone. I was disconnected. I paced the room.

Anxious, afraid. I knew I could not leave. The coup d'état was a deadly, serious situation. I knew all negotiations with Mahmud had fallen apart. The fear of losing my husband left me panic stricken. Why is this happening to me again? I was a widow at thirty, will I be a widow again? What if they never release Wally? What if they killed him?

Feeling severed from any information, I ventured to the lobby. There was chaos with reporters and guests all trying to get news of the coup. Right outside our hotel, bullets were flying. Reporters said president General Zia was trying to hold on to power as uprisings were everywhere. We feared it would get worse. We feared for our safety and those on the plane.

A reporter told me, "When the hijacked plane landed in Bangladesh, General Zia appointed Vice Air Marshal Mahmud to negotiate from the tower. The army was sent to the airport to oversee security freeing the JRA prisoners and the $6 million. When the junior members of the air force got news of the ransom, they staged a coup to get the $6 million. The hijackers held the American banker, John Gabriel near the front window and shot a gun off twice next to his head."

My body almost collapsed. I slumped over holding on to the top of a chair. "Is Gabriel alive?" I whispered.

"No one knows." He answered.

"Does anyone know if Mahmud is alive?" I asked.

Another journalist interjected, "They took Mahmud, hostage. They shot his officer standing right next to him dead. The rebel young Air Force saw the six million dollars in white laundry bags, about as tall as you. They went crazy and started shooting where the Japanese and Bangladesh officers were trying to work out the terms. They murdered most of the people in the room.

"The plane arrived with the money and the nine terrorists released from the jails. Takeo Fukuda, the Japanese Prime Minister, struggled to get the hijackers to accept their request and was on board to deliver the money and terrorists. The Japanese government assigned Ishii as the representative."

The reporter continued, "Okudaira was the Red Army's Prince and was released from Tokyo's prison. Maruoka shot three times in the air, twice to the ground. That started a shooting exchange around six times. Ishii tried to negotiate, but they ignored him. The General tried to get Okudaira to free more passengers. Okudaira came to the plane and went directly into the cockpit. Ishii sought to speak to the Red Army, but they refused to talk to him.

Suddenly, the aircraft moved. The plane was backed up with full power, then moved forward rapidly suddenly, then it stopped. A security officer had stopped the plane."

Ishii saw many dead soldiers with blood all over the airport building. After eight hours throughout the night, the coup settled down. The General was evacuated from the control tower, and he never returned."

Another reporter said, "These maniac Red Army guys are horrible. They demonstrated their disregard for human life in several previous operations. Do you remember the 1972 massacre in Israel's Lod, now called Ben-Gurion airport? They caused that incident along with other brutal killings and hijackings."

Oh no! I didn't know they were the same group that did that!

"I was at the airport," another journalist said, "there was a burst of gunfire at the airport. I saw a sharp firefight. Several army officers shot their own troops. According to some reports, there was shooting on the outskirts of Dacca, besieging several senior officers in the airport terminal building. Confusion engulfed the airport. After about ninety minutes, Radio Bangladesh announced that elements of the army had overthrown the government."

Another journalist said, "I think they protected the Dhaka negotiators not knowing these historic purges that happened in Bangladesh in 1971 when they were fighting a liberation with Pakistan. The hijackers are incredulous; some prisoners refused to fly to Dhaka. Japan sent over prisoners and time was also lost getting the six million dollars."

The hotel manager instructed loudly, "Everyone keep down. People are firing on top of the radio station building right next to us! Stay down or go to your rooms. Stay away from windows, bullets come through windows. I don't want anyone getting hurt!"

The people in the lobby thought they would all be shot. There was more fear displayed in the lobby in that few minutes than I saw on the plane for several days. People were screaming, and others were crying holding their heads in agony.

Wanting to be alone I returned to my room. I needed to talk to my mother. Placing a call to my home took twenty minutes to get through. I was so happy to be speaking to my mother who I loved so much. Mother had a bad heart so I tried to act as strong and calm as I could but I was shaking so hard my voice betrayed me. I gave Mother an update assuring her I was safe, but Wally and the Gabriels were still on the plane. I didn't know if they were going to be freed. She was relieved to know I was off the aircraft. I didn't tell her about the coup. Her health was delicate, and I didn't want her to worry more than she already was. Trying to act calm I asked, "How are my boys doing?"

Mother said, "The boys are well. They are asleep now. Carole, I haven't told them what was happening to you. Everyone is so worried about you. Your picture is on every newspaper front cover all over the world. Larry's cousins Michael and Linda Niven took your boys to the beach house for a few days with their children. Every time they walked past a newsstand they had to distract the boys, so they wouldn't see your picture on the front pages. I think they heard on the television you were on the hijacked plane."

My heart sank. I replied trying to sound cool not to upset my mother, "I always tell my boys the truth. I'm concerned they will find out and think I am dead. Mother, please tell them tomorrow I am safe. It will be easier on them if you answer their questions. Thank you, I am so blessed that you are there watching them."

Falling apart hearing my beloved mother's voice I lost my bravado and started to cry. "Oh Mother, I didn't know how dangerous these people are. I have never seen such evil. They thought we were Jewish and they said we would be the first ones killed. They hate Jews and Americans. I've never known such hatred!" My voice trembled, "What if they kill everyone on the plane? Mother, I'm utterly frightened.

"Keep praying, my Darling. Thank God, you and your children are safe. My goodness, everyone is calling or coming by to help. Your staff has done an excellent job keeping food cooked and everything running smoothly. My Lord, your friends, and family sent so many flowers to the house it feels like a funeral home."

"Let's hope we won't be having one. Oh, it feels so good to talk to you. I received your Western Union you sent to the Ambassador today. Mother, I don't know what to do. I'm very scared, and I don't feel well. I feel out of control and can't understand why this is happening. I love you and hope we get home safely. Thank you for being such a wonderful mother and grandmother. I love you. I'll call you tomorrow. Good night, Mother."

I felt better after hearing my sons were doing well. My mother surprised me about the international news stories and photos plastered over the papers. I had felt abandoned but now realized there must be some negotiations by our state department. That made me feel safer.

CHAPTER ELEVEN

# COUP D'ÉTAT

**A**ir Vice Marshal A.G. Mahmud worked day and night to placate the hijackers, had to manage the terrorism situation, and be in the middle of a coup d'état at the same time!

Years later I learned the details from his book, *My Destiny*. He narrates:

"The dateline for meeting the demands of the hijackers had expired at 4 a.m. that morning. To gain time, I engaged them in various discussions. The hijackers would only speak to me and nobody else. Thus, I had to be available always at the control tower.

"Ultimately, on the 1st of October, a relief plane with six Red Army prisoners, six million US dollars, and about seventy passengers arrived in Dhaka at 11:25 hours. One of

103

the civil aviation officers told me that the relief aircraft did not provide the required manifest. I suspect that the plane could be bringing some commandos for a possible encounter with the hijackers. I instructed the pilot to taxi and park at the other end of the runway furthest from the hijacked aircraft. I also requested Vice Minister Mr. Hajime Ishii to receive the Japanese dignitaries. After the delegation had stepped out of the relief plane, I instructed that the aircraft doors should remain closed and nobody else should be allowed to come out.

"Mr. Ishii wanted to speak to the hijackers himself. The delay in handing over the ransom made the hijackers agitated. I noticed that the aircraft engines were running, and the plane started moving towards the runway. At first, I thought the terrorists might take off and leave Dhaka. But the speed of the plane on the runway clearly showed that they were heading towards the relief aircraft, possibly to forcibly rescue their comrades which would invariably have resulted in bloodshed resulting in chaos. I, therefore, ordered all vehicles to rush and block the runway. The plane could not proceed any further. They threatened to kill American banker, Mr. Gabriel and started firing at our vehicles. By talking to them for about one and a half hours, I calmed them down, and the plane returned to its original position. Thus, sparing the life of Mr. Gabriel. It was agreed that for every million dollars, ten passengers were released. For their jailed comrade named Okudaira, I therefore, ensured that Okudaira was the last person handed over to the hijackers.

"I asked Group Captain Taher Quddus to bring the last prisoner Okudaira to an office on the ground floor, which he did. I told him that we could not allow the hijackers to leave Dhaka with so many passengers. I also said that if my instructions were ignored, they would face dire consequences and would not be allowed to leave. Okudaira told me that he would try to get released as many passengers as possible. This worked. The hijackers only kept 26 passengers and released the rest. The whole exchange was completed by 5:00 am. While the highjack situation was progressing satisfactorily, a dangerous situation was developing inside our forces.

"On 28th of September, there was mutiny in Bogra Cantonment and mutineers were moving towards Dhaka. From 28 September to 2nd October, I was at the control tower, except on two occasions when I attended the cabinet meetings. On the night of October 1st, the troops at the Army Signals Battalion rose in revolt. The battalion was adjacent to Kurmiyola Air Base. The mutineers went over the perimeter wall and started firing in the air, shouting revolutionary slogans. The airmen were asleep in their barracks. The rebels herded the airmen and went to the ordinance depot. They took out arms but did not have ammunition.

"One group took control of the radio. At dawn, a group of airmen entered the airport and started firing indiscriminately at our officers. I was in the office of the DG of civil aviation when a group of airmen took me to the ground floor. Dhaka base commander Group Captain Ansaar Chowdhury was with me. One sergeant, with an automatic gun in his hand, made both of us stand in the middle of the hall and opened fire. Chowdhury dropped dead, and I heard a loud voice shouting 'not the chief.'

The sergeant fired and missed me. I steadily moved towards him and physically grabbed him to calm him down. He was strong and sweating like a pig. He got himself freed from me and went away. A group of airmen escorted me to a room and concealed me. They brought me a Lungi and asked me to changed my clothes, which I did. At this stage, these airmen left, and a new set of airmen came. They did not utter a word to me nor spoke among themselves. The first thing they did was disconnect the telephone line. By this time the dawn was breaking. Through the window, I could see some troop movement. Suddenly, the door opened, and there stood before me an army captain. He and his men took me out of the room and started running across the runway. I was too exhausted and could not keep up with them. The soldiers helped me to keep pace. I saw some airmen roaming around with arms.

"The captain who rescued me was Sadeq Hassan Rumi, who later became general and retired. I learned about the havoc the armed airmen had caused and the death of so many officers. Mutiny at Bogra took place on the 28th September. The air force officers on duty at the airport were shot and killed just before dawn on 2nd October 1977.

"Coming back to the hijackers, I had a meeting with Okudaira and told him if more passengers were not released they would not be allowed to depart from Dhaka. This meeting worked. Earlier, the Japanese ambassador said that the Algerian government had agreed to provide temporary asylum to the hijackers. We provided necessary maps and charts for their flight to Algeria. They left Dhaka with 26 passengers bringing an end to the crisis. I was not present at the airport when they left.

"On the morning of 3rd October, I along with some troops from the 9th Division went to Kurmitola to disarm the airmen. All of them came out and gathered in a disciplined manner. I asked them to surrender their arms. One by one all the arms were deposited in front of me. Then, I went to my office and took stock of the situation. There was gloom among officers. The mutineers killed eleven officers."

# CHAPTER TWELVE

# END OF COUP

**D**uring the night Mahmud was evacuated from the control tower and never returned. The junior air force wanted to keep the six million dollars and decided to take over the country. They shot the army officers killing several in the airport and more soldiers on top of the radio station next to my hotel.

While everyone slept, General Zia called on his army to go into the young air force living quarters and kill all of his airmen, all two hundred of them, since he didn't know who was on his side or not. It was a dramatic and horrible ending to the coup. It is worthy to mention that all 560 of the mutineers were hanged for their crimes. The government tried to keep the killing of the air force a secret so the press wouldn't tell the world, exposing it as a "Banana Republic" but soon it was uncovered. By morning the coup was over, and communications with the terrorist began again.

Feeling helpless, I called my dearest girlfriend since junior high school, Pam Packer Scott who is a minister and asked her to pray for John, Wally, Agnes and safety for all of us. So many people murdered I knew her prayers would help their souls make the transition easier. Pam always answers my calls and has powerful prayers. I felt better after talking and praying with her. All I could do is wait and pray for their safety.

The hijackers released several more passengers and a stewardess. The JRA comrades and money were now on board their plane. They released most of the passengers, but kept Wally and several more Americans. The Ambassador called me that John and Agnes Gabriel were released. The Red Cross carried John on a stretcher off the plane. I met the Red Cross Van at the hospital and told the doctors that John had prostrate problems. They gave him a catheter, and his urine was black in color. I was worried he was too far-gone and would die. He needed antibiotics. I asked the Ambassador to please have the American doctor treat him.

John was in terrible shape, deliriously out of his mind. He kept mumbling, "He held me in the cockpit while the shooting was going on outside the plane. He told me he was going kill me. Then the head guy shot the gun right by my ear. When he fired the gun, I thought I was shot. I fell... passed out."

The doctor gave him a sedative to sleep.

Agnes was my primary concern now that the doctor attended to John. She was always patient, helping her husband every minute, not ever thinking about herself. Once I knew John was taken care of, I insisted she let the doctor take her blood pressure and see if she was well enough to leave the hospital.

Our Ambassador's driver took us from the hospital to the hotel. I took off Agnes' clothes to be laundered. I drew her a warm bath and helped her into the bathtub. Being so weak she almost fell several times. I washed her back and hair as if she were my little girl. This amazing woman stood silently by like a rock, never wanting the limelight, and always giving it to her husband. She had never been to Europe and was so happy to be on our trip. I felt so sorry that it ended so horribly.

Agnes was exhausted from worrying about John that she didn't resist me helping her. I gave her a kimono to wear and ordered soup for dinner. She was trembling so much I had to spoon-feed her a few sips, but she couldn't eat. I poured her champagne, which she liked and later gave her some hot tea. Pulling back the covers, I suggested she go to bed. Agonized, she let me rub her back, and I stayed with her until she fell asleep. Assuring her she was safe in the hotel I slept on her couch to be near her. I didn't want her to wake up and be frightened. Poor Agnes had spent four days with the hijackers under the threat of death and watched her husband dragged to the cockpit to be killed.

The next morning after Agnes awakened, we loaded the car's trunk with soft drinks and food for John and other released passengers in the hospital. We tried to make John comfortable, and he stayed another night in the hospital. Agnes stayed with John constantly watching over him like a guardian angel.

The hotel lobby was teeming with reporters and released passengers. Our Ambassador still didn't know anything new. No one was allowed to go to the airport. The reporters were not allowed near it. I didn't feel like talking to the press, so Agnes and I went to our rooms. I trembled worrying if my husband would ever get off the plane before the hijackers flew away.

I needed to call my Washington friends that might talk some sense into these madmen. I called one of our best friends, Joe Cerrell, the guru for politicians, asking on Wally's behalf for help from Washington D.C. I didn't call President Carter, because I didn't know him personally, but I called Past Vice President Hubert Humphrey, a close friend of John's and Wally's. He assured me he would talk to the President. Humphrey had dinner with Wally and me several times, and we gave him a fundraiser in our home. I always liked Hubert Humphrey and felt he would get involved. He said he would do all he could to help get Wally released.

I spoke to Ronald Reagen who was a special friend of mine and California Legislator John Burton also Wally's close friend. I tried calling everyone I knew on both sides of the political parties asking them to help get my husband released. I asked if they could bargain with the gangsters... perhaps ask before they gave them fuel for their escape, to release my husband? It worked! The tower told the hijackers, "No fuel unless you release Walter Karabian." At the last minute, they let Wally off the plane!

When I saw my husband Wally, I cried from relief. He looked tired. Most of his hair had turned white. He barely spoke, took a shower, ate, and crawled into the bed holding me close all night.

# CHAPTER THIRTEEN

# LAST DAY
# OF TERROR

**J**apanese Air Lines staff organized the passengers to depart for the airport. They gathered in the lobby. I sat on a green silk couch, holding the little bags that each person had entrusted to me. Each one, shyly approached me to gather their belongings. I had spread some of them on the table so they could recognize some of the cloth that held their personal effects. Most didn't speak English but they thanked me for guarding their things. I was grateful that I was able to help them, albeit in a small way.

The following day John, Agnes, Wally, and I drove to the airport in the Ambassador's car. Driving to the airport was hellacious. The powerful monsoon rains almost washed away our car. Having never been in a monsoon before, we were impressed by its ferocity. We had to jump out, wade to the curb, and be transferred into the Ambassador's large van shuttling us to the airport.

At the same time the hijackers flew away keeping a few Americans with them until they finished their flight to Algeria. They wanted to avoid their plane being shot down over Israel with twenty-six hostages, six million dollars, and their nine comrades.

Our flight left Bangladesh to Bangkok where representatives from the King and Queen of Thailand welcomed us in a private room. They gave us little presents and offered their condolences for our ordeal.

We continued our flight to Tokyo.

Arriving in Japan, the airport was filled with hundreds of people with more little gifts of perfume, cakes, and handkerchiefs. I was surprised how many people recognized me and remembered me from being on television in the series *National Velvet*. I had a large fan club in Japan. They remembered me and were embarrassed that we had to endure the hijacking.

John Gabriel was too ill to continue flying, so we stayed two more days in Tokyo waiting for John to gain strength enough to return to America. More gifts came to our hotel from Japanese well-wishers. I bought John and Agnes a few toiletries and tried to help them as much as I could. Our first night in Japan we were awakened by an earthquake that frightened me all over again. It felt like Godzilla was shaking our hotel building. When I called down to the desk, I asked, "Did we just had an earthquake?"

He answered casually as if I were asking for room service, "Yes Madam, Japan has them all the time."

CHAPTER FOURTEEN

# HOME

**S**eeing the beautiful coastline of San Francisco my happiness to be safely back in America changed to anger. I became furious that these murderers had kidnapped us, taken away our dignity and treated us like animals.

Family and friends greeted us as we walked into our home. Our home in Los Angeles looked like a funeral parlor with exquisite flower arrangements. The sweet smell made me feel sick, and I asked my friends to take the arrangements to the Children's hospital.

I remember holding my sons, Sean and Ryan all afternoon and evening. I couldn't let go of them. I kept them with me in my bed that night afraid to let them out of my sight.

The telephone rang constantly and press news channels called trying to arrange television interviews which I did do later. I became the spokeswoman for the Airplane Pilots Association worldwide who demanded more metal detectors in all the airports. They were going to strike if stricter protection was not enforced.

The next Saturday Wally and I attended our alma mater, the University of Southern California, to watch a football game. Halfway through the game, I started to bleed and then hemorrhaged. I was rushed to the hospital where I lost my baby. The doctor said the shock from the terror sent a rush of adrenaline that killed our baby boy, Krikor.

The disappointment of losing my baby and the recovery from our distress sent me into a depression for several weeks. On Christmas day, my husband and I decided to not talk about the hijacking experience anymore. We wanted to move forward, but the nightmares from our ordeal never left me. Now, after forty years I write about my experience as a catharsis as I slowly dredge up those horrific days as a captive.

# CHAPTER FIFTEEN

# WHAT HAPPENED TO THE TERRORISTS?

**A**fter a long 24-year manhunt, Osamu Marouka, 45 years old was finally arrested and put in Tokyo's prison for life. The Japanese police immediately arrested him upon entering Japan from Hong Kong.

Japanese news said the police suspected that Mr. Maruoka may have been planning an attack on the Seoul Olympics. Mr. Maruoka had reservations on a flight to Seoul, and police said they had discovered a newsletter sent to Japanese Red Army sympathizers denouncing the Seoul Olympics as a "new counterrevolutionary ring" linking South Korea with Japan and the United States. The police would not confirm this account.

The Japanese Red Army emerged in the late 1960's and supported Palestinian groups, massacring 26 people in the 1972 attack at the airport, now the Ben-Gurion International Airport. Two of the three attackers also died. The third was released by Israel in 1985 in a prisoner exchange and went to Libya.

Since 1972, the Japanese Red Army has mounted several other attacks, including hijacking a Japan Air Lines plane from Amsterdam to Tokyo in 1973, attacking the Japanese Embassy in Kuala Lumpur, Malaysia, in 1975, and hijacking a Japan Air Lines flight from Bombay to Dhaka, Bangladesh, in 1977.

The police offered few details of how they tracked down Mr. Maruoka. The police say that about 40 members remain active, many in the Middle East.

Okudaira's location is unknown.

# CHAPTER SIXTEEN

# QUEEN SHIGENOBU FUSAKO

**I**t's hard to realize that the three years before the hijacking when I was in Beirut driving past the fenced in Palestinian ghetto the leader, queen Fusako of the Japanese Red Army was hiding, moving from one Arab camp to another.

Queen Shigenobu Fusako, born on September 28, 1945, is a Japanese founder and former leader of now disbanded Red Army. She lived in Beirut, Lebanon, yet was born in the Setagaya ward of Tokyo. Her father was a teacher at a temple school for poor village children in the Japanese Kyushu region after the First World War. He became a major in the Imperial Japanese Army and was dispatched to Manchuria, a region under Japanese control before and during World War II.

After high school, Shigenobu attended Meiji University receiving a BA in Political Economy and History. She joined the student movement that was protesting the increase in tuition fees, and this led her to activism in the leftist student movement of the 1960s. She rose the ranks of the movement to become one of its top leaders.

Shigenobu had been a leading member of the Red Army Faction in Japan whose roots lay in the militant new-left Communist League. They set up their group, declaring war on the state in September 1969. Fusako Shigenobu left Japan with only a handful of dedicated people, but her group is reported to have had 40 members at its height. In February 1971, she and Tsuyoshi Okudaira went to the Middle East to make international contacts for the Japanese Red Army Faction. Shigenobu remained in the Middle East for more than 30 years.

Her move was part of International Revolutionary Solidarity, with the idea that revolutionary movements should cooperate and eventually lead to a global socialist revolution. Her destination was Lebanon, and her aim was to support the Palestinian cause. She initially joined the Popular Front for the Liberation of Palestine (PFLP) as a volunteer, but eventually, the Japanese Red Army became an independent group. Shigenobu returned to Japan sometime during July 2000. She was sentenced to 20 years in prison on March 8, 2006, and received a final verdict from the Supreme Court in 2010 with the same sentence terms.

In December 2008, Shigenobu was diagnosed with colon and intestinal cancer. She had three operations to remove them.

She is living in Hachioji Medical Prison. Fusako Shigenobu is the mother of Japanese national Mai now May, Shigenobu, a journalist. Mai is trying to get her mother released to die at home.

CHAPTER SEVENTEEN

# MAI SHIGENOBU

**I**n February 2016 Naeem Mohaiemen a film producer, artist, and researcher using essays, films, and photography invited me to attend the Film Festival in Newcastle, England. He presented his film, *United Red Army, The Young Man Was, Part 1.* It covered our hijacking in 1977. Naeem is a graduate of Columbia University and a recipient of a Guggenheim Fellowship. It was the rigorous research that Naeem Mohaiemen accomplished restoring old films and news coverage from our hijacking that prevented the facts from disappearing forever.

Mohaiemen arranged after the showing of his film to have a Q&A with Air Vice Marshall Mahmud and himself in Bangladesh on SKYPE. I was thrilled to speak to them and to especially again thank Air Vice Marshall Mahmud for saving our lives. He is such a humble and courageous man.

Mai Shigenobu, the terrorist queen's daughter, was scheduled to show her film the next night. When I met the terrorist Queen's daughter in the living room of the hotel in Newcastle, I was filled with mixed emotions. Part of me was curious to find out about her life; another part of me wanted to smash her face, yell that she was a promoter of terrorism and should be ashamed of her mother and her father.

A writer from *the Guardian* was fussing over her as if she were a star, and I wondered why they gave her so much attention. Later I read that she was a journalist in Lebanon. We had a brief hello, and I left to have dinner and go to bed. I couldn't sleep remembering the horror of my hijacking experience. I tossed and turned during the night angry that I was sleeping in the same hotel with the daughter of the Queen of the Japanese Red Army!

May as she now spells her name, not Mai, is a good-looking woman in her forties. She had just arrived from Beirut and was giving a speech after the showing of her film the next night of the film festival, *Children of the Revolution.*

Mai was not a citizen of any country until March 2001, when she received Japanese citizenship. Shigenobu lived most of her childhood years in Palestinian refugee camps in Lebanon; her mother, Fusako Shigenobu, was absent for months at a time, and her mother's comrades in the Japanese Red Army, Arab friends, and supporters raised Mei in those periods.

Mai's mother became wanted by the INTERPOL in 1974. Mai was forced to move frequently and use aliases to evade reprisals by her mother's enemies. Her early education was in several schools in Lebanon and studied journalism at the Lebanese University as well as going to the American University of Beirut in Lebanon. During those years, she learned to speak fluent Arabic and English, but hid her knowledge of Japanese, fearing that if her identity as Fusako Shigenobu's daughter were to become known publicly, her mother might be captured.

Mai came out of hiding after her mother was captured in Osaka, and visited Japan for the first time in April 2001, making her the first child of a Japanese Red Army member to return to Japan in five years. She began working as an English teacher in a school in Tokyo.

Mai later became an anchor on Japanese cable television channel, *Asahi New Star's*, and United Arab Emirates' Arabic satellite channel, *Tokyo correspondent*, reporting in Arabic about Japan.

Mai Shigenobu is a supporter of Palestinian statehood and a critic of Israel. She views her mother's actions with pride, to the point of stating that she considers her a role model.

The next evening, I listened to her talk after viewing her film. She talked about her life in the Palestinian camps always running from authorities. She tried to justify the group's terrorist activities by making the claim that in the 70s and 80s people had very different "moral values," "sensibilities and ways of thinking." She implied that her mother's sentence should be rendered invalid. Echoing her mother's claim that since the criminal acts carried out had political aims, she should not be convicted but rather offered a "political way out."

She said, "There were no means of gaining media attention, and with today's media and communication, other venues prove far more efficient."

Mai kept calling them Revolutionaries and their intention was not to kill or harm anyone.

I wanted to scream, "Liar, tell that to all the families of the people they killed!" I controlled my emotions and sat there stoically, but I could feel my body seething, burning with anger.

Mai said, "I spent my first eight or nine years, in a commune, an island of mostly Japanese Red Army members living in various Palestinian camps filled with refugees who shared the group's aim of an independent Palestinian state. Mother would often leave for months at a time, and I pleaded to be taken along, only to be told it was too cold. During my mother's long absences, other Japanese Red Army comrades filled in, helping me with homework, making school lunches, putting me to bed. I consider them part of my family.

"The group was very organized, with schedules and rotating chore lists." Mai said. "The most significant decisions were made by consensus, with even the opinion of the youngest considered during discussions and lively debates.

"Over time, the group's hope of the world changing gradually faded, but its members organized their home along three revolutionary pillars: solidarity, self-sacrifice, and self-criticism. Each day," Mai told us, "members assembled to consider and criticize their mistakes and suggest ways avoiding them in the future."

After her talk, I was driven back to our hotel and several of us enjoyed a glass of port in the bar before retiring. She joined us. We discussed at great length her experience. I asked her questions, "Are you able to trust anyone now?"

She said, "no."

"Having to lie all your young life must have been very hard on you," I said.

She said, "I didn't know any other way of life, so it didn't seem too difficult for me."

I asked, "Were you able to have any friends?"

"I had the other Red Army children as my friends, and we keep in touch."

"Aren't you ashamed that your parents were so ruthless?"

"No," she replied, "It was different then. There was no internet to get your ideas heard, so they had to be aggressive."

She never knew who her father was until recently. When Mai visited her mother in jail the last time, she knew she had cancer, so her mother told Mai his name. Mai has never revealed who he is but is still very close to the Palestinian movement, speaking out against Israel.

When I first met this attractive young woman, I felt rage in me and wanted to slap her to punish her for her mother's deeds. The rush of such primitive emotion surprised me. I listened to her story and heard how difficult her life was always being on the run. She had to lie to everyone all her life. She had to reinvent herself many times a year and move from school to school. She could never tell her real name. Her life was always hiding from place to place in Lebanon from the authorities. Her existence of never having a safe home, never keeping friends, not being with her mother for extended periods of time must have left her lonely.

Her eyes were smoldering dark and barely any expression. She was cold as steel, and I knew we could never be friends. I wanted to stay away from her because I saw no inner light inside her heart. As we were sitting across from each other, a strange thing happened to me. After hearing her sad story of growing up on the run avoiding authorities, I began to feel sorry for her realizing it wasn't her fault that she was born into those unusual circumstances.

I remember praying for her soul to be enlightened and given understanding and peace. When I went up to my room, the fire of rage in me seemed to subside. I felt like there was the healing of a painful wound that stuck inside me, buried so many years ago. I didn't realize before the Film Festival why Naeem Mohaiemen invited me to attend the film festival. I had said yes, believing in Naeem's work, I now know God put me in the place of opportunity to meet my nemesis face to face and forgive her. God works miracles all the time. Being released safely from the terrorists was a miracle. Meeting Mai and having to face my demons, was a miracle for it has softened my heart. I realize how young these terrorists were and I can understand it better. I have forgiven them.

It was important for me to write this story now since so many people are facing fear and starvation from the actions of the terrorists all over the world. I want my readers to understand how these life-changing experiences never leave us, and we are all emotionally scarred from them.

When one keeps fear inside your mind for so many years as I did after the hijacking, it is surprising how one's body reacts when something happens that reminds you of the terrible incident.

*Carole with Mai Shigenobu*

Later I studied the backgrounds of the Chinese revolution and then the Japanese revolution in the 60's while American kids my age were demonstrating at Berkeley and other college campuses against the Viet Nam war. I finally, after years of not understanding their intentions, realize everyone wanted to express their frustration and to do something to change the way they were living as a result of political ideology.

*CHAPTER EIGHTEEN*

# WHAT HAPPENED TO THE REST OF THE JAPANESE RED ARMY?

**F**usako Shigenobu, founder and leader, was arrested in Osaka, Japan, November 2000. Japan accused Shigenobu of orchestrating attacks, kidnappings, and hijackings. At one time labeled by critics as "the most feared female terrorist in the world," she helped plan the 1972 attack at Lod Airport. A court in Tokyo sentenced her in February 2006 to serve 20 years in prison.

**Haruo Wakō,** the former leader, arrested February 1997.

**Osamu Maruoka,** former leader and the hijacker of two aircraft, was arrested in November 1987 in Tokyo after entering Japan on a forged passport. Given a life sentence, he died in prison on May 29, 2011.

**Yū Kikumura** was arrested with explosives on the New Jersey Turnpike in 1988 and served over 18 years of a 30-year prison sentence in the United States. In April 2007, Kikumura was released from US incarceration and immediately arrested upon his return to Japan. He was released in October 2007.

**Yoshimi Tanaka** was sentenced to 12 years for the Yodo-go hijacking that ended in North Korea.

**Yukiko Ekida,** the former member of East Asia Anti-Japan Armed Front and a long-time JRA leader, was arrested in March 1995 in Romania and subsequently deported to Japan. She received a sentence of 20 years for attempted murder and violating the explosives law in a series of bombings targeting large companies in 1974 and 1975. The trial of Ekida was originally started in 1975 but was suspended when she was released from prison in 1977. Her release was part of a deal with the Japanese Red Army during the hijacking of a Japanese airliner to Bangladesh.

**Kōzō Okamoto** is the only survivor of the group of three Guerrillas attacking the Israeli Lod airport in 1972, now called Ben Gurion International Airport. He stayed jailed in Israel, but in May 1985, Okamoto was set free in an exchange of prisoners between Israeli and Palestinian forces. Subsequently, he was imprisoned in Lebanon for three years for forging visas and passports. The Lebanese authorities granted Okamoto asylum in 1999 because he was alleged to have been tortured in prison in Israel.

**Masao Adachi, Kazuo Tohira, Haruo Wak** , and **Mariko Yamamoto** were also imprisoned in Lebanon on charges of forgery yet were sent to Jordan. As the Jordanian authorities refused to allow them into Jordan, they were handed over to Japan.

**Kuniya Akagi,** a collaborator of the JRA, was arrested after returning to Osaka from Pyongyang via Beijing to be questioned over the kidnapping of three Japanese nationals in Europe by North Korean spies in the 1980s.

**Hiroshi Sensei,** a JRA militant, living in the Philippines, was arrested by the Integrated National Police as part of anti-terrorist measures to prevent terrorist incidents from taking place in the Seoul Olympic games after being tipped off by the Japanese National Police Agency

**Kunio Bando** was a key member and is still on Interpol's wanted list. He may have taken refuge in the Philippines in the year 2000.

# REFERENCES

*MY DESTINY* by AIR VICE-MARSHAL MAHMUD

Sound Clips from NAEEM MOHAIEMEN

Shigenobu Fusako's real daughter published autobiography, Tokyo Broadcasting System, 2002-06-15, archived from the original on June 27, 2007, retrieved 2007-09-14

In 2008, artist Anicka Yi and architect Maggie Peng created a perfume dedicated to Shigenobu, called *Shigenobu Twilight*. In 2010, Shigenobu, and her daughter Mai were featured in the documentary *Children of the Revolution*.

2009: A Personal History of the Japanese Red Army: Together with Palestine. *Jump up*

*Shigenobu Fusako*. "Japanese Red Army leader arrested." BBC. November 8, 2000. Retrieved January 16, 2016.

Japanese Red Army Leader Gets 20 Years in Prison, Palestine Press, February 23, 2007

McNeill, David (July 4, 2014). "Mai Shigenobu's words continue the fight for her mother's cause." The Japan Times. Retrieved January 16, 2016.

In 2010, Shigenobu and her daughter Mai were featured in the documentary *Children of the Revolution*, which premiered at the International Documentary Festival Amsterdam.

# ACKNOWLEDGEMENTS

AIR VICE-MARSHAL MAHMUD: Thank you for the hours of negotiations saving all the passengers' lives.

NAEEM MOHAIEMEN: Without Naeem's tenacity and research most of the history of the hijacking would have been lost. Thank you for sending me to Newcastle, England to learn more of their plight.

PEOPLE OF BANGLADESH: Who made our stay as comfortable as possible and fought to save our lives and their army and air force for their great sacrifice.

OUR AMERICAN AMBASSADOR, ED MASTERS and HIS STAFF AND OUR CIA OFFICERS: Who help us stay informed and safe from harm.

ANTON TROY for working with me and interpreting my designs for the cover with the Argentine artist DIEGO TRIPODI.

MY MOTHER AND COUSINS MICHAEL AND LINDA NIVEN: who took care of my sons during our hijacking.

MARIE FRILLICI who spent hours finding my articles and photos for this book.

My LOVING HUSBAND, JERRY VANIER who patiently gave me the time to write this book and held me in his arms when I had meltdowns reliving these horrible events.

# BIOGRAPHICAL
# HISTORY

**C**arole Wells began working as an actress in films, television and musical and dramatic theater at 12 years old. At seventeen, she sang the coloratura solo in Puccini's operatic *Messa di Gloria* at the Hollywood Bowl and co-starred in the television series *National Velvet*, and later, Pistols 'n Petticoats. She has appeared in 12 motion pictures, over 100 television shows and has traveled all over the world singing in various venues for such audiences as royalty and government leaders. In her travels, she learned how fantastic it was to be an American. It is important to respect and listen to older people, get as much education as possible, travel abroad, and study languages.

As a young girl, Carole spent part of her vacations working in her father's doctor's office, where she learned empathy for the less fortunate. A major part of her adult life was spent in the service of others, working mainly for physically disabled and emotionally disturbed children.

Carole studied sound therapy for many years and introduced the scientist who invented voice-activated technology to the University of Southern California School of Medicine. This new technology gave mobility to thousands of paralyzed children. As president of the Las Floristas Charity, Carole helped raise money to build the Center for Applied Rehabilitation Therapy at Rancho Los Amigos in Southern California.

She has been involved in children's causes and charities over the last forty-five years.

She was an active member on the Board of the Hollywood High Alumni Association for eighteen years. She served as Vice President for five years and President for two years helping under privileged students obtain scholarships for college.

During and after the Vietnam War, she sang and entertained paraplegic soldiers each month—traveling to the Veteran's Hospitals in San Francisco, Long Beach, and San Diego. She helped start the first Wheel Chair Olympics and Special Olympics. Both the City and County of Los Angeles honored her with their Humanitarian Awards.

Carole has been active in politics since she was twenty-one, giving speeches for two Republican United States Presidents and two Senators.

Studying Metaphysics and religions for ten years, Carole learned as a young child she was able to read people's auras and to diagnose their health problems. She is a Medical Intuitive and has helped hundreds of people regain their health. She conducted each week a Meditation evening teaching people how to understand the science of meditation for many years.

Seeing life as an adult since the sixties, she learned that the important thing isn't what happens to us; it is how we deal with what happens! Carole tries to be an example of unconditional love and doing no harm to others. She has written several articles on women's rights and how some religions treat women in a despicable manner.

Carole work has been published in ten books of other writers and published a young person's adventure story, Amberella and now has released Hijacked …an eye witness account of evil. Her next book is about her glamourous life in the sixties being a television and movie star married to oil scion Larry Doheny of California.

Carole is now co-writing and staring in a short film "Fallen Leaves" to be released in 2018.

Carole has four children and six grandchildren whom she enjoys being with as often as possible.

To find all her movie and television credits, please look up IMBD or visit her website: carolewells.com.

Made in the USA
Columbia, SC
05 October 2018